THE
Old West
BAKING BOOK

BY Lon Walters

PHOTOGRAPHS BY Gene Balzer

NORTHLAND PUBLISHING

To my best friend and life partner, Margi.

Cover: Chuckwagon and camp, Greene Cattle Co.

Clip art courtesy of Windmill Press at
2147 Windmill View Road, El Cajon, California 92020

Text © 1996 by Lon Walters
All photographs © 1996 by Gene Balzer, with the following exceptions:
Courtesy of Northern Arizona University Cline Library: page 99
(John Wesley Powell Display Collection) and page 170 (Philip Johnston Collection).
Courtesy of the Heard Museum: page 67. Courtesy of Arizona Historical Society:
cover and pages vi and 71; pages iii and 28 (Barnes Collection). Courtesy of Sharlot Hall Museum:
page 17. Courtesy of Museum of Northern Arizona: pages 3, 39,
and 127 (Earle R. Forrest Collection); page 151, 172.
All rights reserved.

www.northlandpub.com

FIRST IMPRESSION, 1996
Composed in the United States of America
Printed in Hong Kong
10 09 08 07 06 05 04 03   10 9 8 7 6 5

Library of Congress Catalog Card Number 95-23399
Cataloging-in-Publication Data

Walters, Lon.
The Old West baking book / by Lon Walters; photographs by Gene Balzer.
p. cm.
ISBN 0-87358-637-9
Includes bibliographic references (p.   ) and index.
1. Baking. 2. Cookery, American—Western style. I. Title.
TX763.W33 1995
641.8'15—dc20   95-23399

Contents

Introduction

⁓

IVING IN THE OLD WEST WAS BOTH A DREAM AND A HORROR. Clear skies and the chance for a new beginning induced tens of thousands who had never gone more than a few blocks from home to travel through miles of hostile territory and parched lands and to undergo untold hardships. They set out to establish new communities and new lives as cowboys, miners, and settlers in new territories. Many mixed well with the current residents; many did not. The successful relationships some made with Native Americans and the environment proved fruitful as their cultures merged and their traditions blended.

Native Americans introduced settlers and cowboys to spices, fruits, and an array of other local food items. With the same spirit that brought them to the West, more imaginative cooks used these indigenous materials to create wonderful meals and baked goods in an otherwise forbidding environment.

Unfortunately, the creative blending and baking of the nineteenth century has given way to megamarket fluff and mass-packaged baked goods. Convenience aside, we have little appreciation for our early ancestors' efforts to make even the most basic foods interesting. Despite our capacity to bake in the world's most advanced and well-equipped home kitchens, we often do less than a pioneer did with just a campfire.

As we step back to see how this was done, stories and trivia will keep the reading light, fun, and perhaps a valuable learning experience. It was an exciting project to research; I hope you have as much fun as I did in sharing the baking with your family and friends.

Chuckwagon and camp, Greene Cattle Co.

Extraordinary
Biscuits &
Quick Breads

Camp for lunch in Santa Fe Canyon, ca. 1900.

Quick Breads: The Real Gold of the Old West

DELIGHTFULLY LIGHT AND SLIGHTLY SWEET, THERE IS NOTHING better than a piping hot slice of quick bread with a cup of coffee or tea. Quick breads have been around for a hundred and fifty years or so with few alterations to the recipes and little change in the utter joy of finishing one to the last crumb.

Quick breads came about in the mid-nineteenth century as a result of experiments with leavening agents (which make breads rise). Baking soda and baking powder were so successful and fast, they were marketed in England as "yeast powder."

This newly discovered "yeast powder" was double acting, meaning the chemical would react both when mixed with liquid and when heated in the oven. The gas produced by the powder would get caught in the gluten, or protein strands, causing the whole mix to rise.

Although it has little in common with living yeast (except for gas production), baking powder began to be substituted in bread and biscuits by bakers in Europe and the populated East Coast of America. It was so easy to use that small batches of bread could be made; and since things happened much faster in the mix, it saved considerable time over baking the yeasted variety.

Pioneers, ranch hands, and chuckwagon cooks discovered this too. A number of early cookbooks and Old West journals made reference to "yeast powder" being a wonderful substitute for saleratus, a common leavening agent of the era.

Saleratus was commercially produced and distributed in small packages. For bakers without access to the corner store, it could also be fashioned at home. However, both techniques resulted in questionable product consistency.

Pictured from top are Corn Muffins (page 34), Whole Wheat–Date Loaf (page 25), and Corn Dodgers (page 35).

Much like basic baking soda, saleratus needed an acid (like sour milk) to be effective. But unlike baking soda, saleratus' strength was so unpredictable, it was a risky proposition to expect any baked products to come out remotely similar in size and texture twice in a row.

Native Americans made saleratus from wood ash. Their process and ingredients were reasonably consistent, so their product was more predictable and was used with some effectiveness in various baked corn goods.

But with the birth of new powders, and the increasingly sophisticated distribution of products throughout the Old West, it became unnecessary to settle for less than the best.

A whole new world of possibilities for consistent baked goods was now available to everyone. Rules for making quick breads are generally opposite those of yeast-leavened breads. Where patience may be a virtue with yeast, quick breads suffer with slow bakers.

They are called quick breads because of the short time to blend and bake. Nothing destroys a good quick bread recipe faster than too much time mixing and baking.

Quick breads want a light touch. This may well be the hardest habit for yeast bread bakers to change. Overbeating of quick breads stretches what little gluten is in the mix, and gas formed by the baking powder and baking soda escapes from the batter. This produces smaller, heavier loaves rivaling building blocks.

Also, while yeast breads stay fresh for days on the kitchen shelf, quick breads stale in about twenty-four hours. Bagging in an airtight wrapper can extend shelf life a bit, but it seriously affects taste.

After all this aggravation, why make quick breads?

As Old West residents discovered, they remain the quickest and easiest loaves and rolls to prepare. Even bakers with rocks for hands could assemble a quick breads, for the less you did, the better they baked. They were truly perfect trail companions.

And creative spirits could mix virtually anything in the batter without fear. Lastly—as noted in dozens of pioneer's personal journals—they are incredibly tasty.

A few rules to remember for assembling quick breads in modern kitchens:

- Do not, repeat, do not even dream of using a food processor to prepare the recipes. The product will be hard and dense unless you have a lightning quick hand atop the on/off switch.
- Do not overmix. Stir the batter by wooden spoon until the dry ingredients are moistened or the result will be the same as using a food processor. Handle as little as possible.
- Don't be afraid to add goodies. Raisins, apple chunks, blueberries, etc., blend well in the mix and add excitement to your quick breads.
- Smaller biscuits are usually better than larger ones due to the very hot oven and short baking time.
- Preheat the oven. A cold oven or long baking will ruin your creation.
- Place quick breads in the oven as soon as they are mixed. The rising action begins immediately after the liquid is added to the recipe and nothing is gained by waiting.
- During baking, splitting and cracking tops on quick breads are OK and, in fact, are preferred. While they indicate some major problems in yeast breads, not true here.

Here are a few classic recipes for quick breads baked on the range. Enjoy.

Originating in Europe, this recipe came to be called "American Baking Powder Biscuits" in the colonies. However, you may recognize the more popular name, scone. By any label, scones have been one of the most popular quick breads for generations. The recipe was carried into the Old West by pioneers who simply couldn't live without the delightful biscuit. The mix was baked in a large Dutch oven placed directly into the campfire. Because they are a bit firmer in texture than "range" biscuits, handling them on the run was much easier, and they were certainly a grand treat for pioneers who had been bumping along in a wooden wagon for twelve hours.

Baking Powder Biscuits

BAKING TIME: *15–20 minutes*
OVEN TEMPERATURE: *400 degrees*

> *2 cups all-purpose flour*
> *1 tablespoon baking powder*
> *3 tablespoons granulated sugar*
> *⅛ teaspoon salt*
> *½ cup butter or margarine*
> *2 eggs, beaten*
> *½ cup milk or cream*

In a large bowl, mix all dry ingredients: flour, baking powder, sugar, and salt. Cut in butter with a knife or pastry blade until the mixture resembles a coarse meal. Do not overmix. Add eggs and milk, stirring with a fork and blending until the dry ingredients are just moistened. Next, you have two options: 1) scoop pieces of batter in 3-ounce rounds (about half the size of a tennis ball) and place onto a well-greased sheet pan, or 2) place the whole mix into a well-greased large cake pan, 8-inch or 9-inch, and spread it evenly. Bake in a preheated oven until the top is golden brown (about 15–20 minutes).

Serve with butter, hot out of the oven. The leftovers will keep for about 3 days.

VARIATIONS
‿ Add ½ cup of raisins, currants, or dates.
‿ Add ¼ teaspoon almond extract or

(continued on following page)

½ teaspoon vanilla with the cream. Before baking, sprinkle the top with slivered almonds.

∽ Add ½ cup blueberries (well drained, or better yet, frozen), and fold in as the very last step.

∽ Add ¼ cup of shredded cheese, your favorite variety.

∽ Add any other precooked (and drained) items you like—chopped sausage, crushed bacon, etc. Make it *your* recipe.

THE DUTCH OVEN

Even if cash-poor ranchers of the Old West coveted a rack of shiny pots and pans, preparation standards of the day didn't allow fixing a meal with anything but the most basic cookware. Space was also a major consideration in any ranch kitchen and especially on board the revered chuck wagon.

One tool rose to the occasion above all others—the Dutch oven. Developed in the early 1700s, this heavy cast-iron pot was found in virtually every kitchen in the Old West by the mid-1800s. With just one kettle, a range cook could fry, steam, or bake foods. With few spices available, ingenious kitchen hands found that cooking food in their own juices produced incredible flavors. A Dutch oven handled this task perfectly.

Constructed of heavy cast iron, it sat on three legs about one inch high. The lid was recessed and flanged to keep coals from mixing with the contents. Depending on depth, it could hold from one to ten gallons. Baking and cooking was a simple task. Clear hot campfire embers to about an inch or so high, place the Dutch oven in the middle, and cover the oven with the remaining embers. The surrounding heat baked biscuits and other popular dishes to perfection. It was so versatile that the lid could be inverted and used as a griddle.

Apple-Corn Loaf

BAKING TIME: *20–25 minutes*
OVEN TEMPERATURE: *425 degrees*

> *1 large apple, diced*
> *½ cup granulated sugar*
> *½ cup corn meal*
> *1½ cups all-purpose flour*
> *½ teaspoon salt*
> *2 teaspoons baking powder*
> *1 egg, beaten*
> *1 cup milk*
> *4 tablespoons butter, melted*

*C*reativity with cornmeal abounded in pioneer times because without some kind of spicing or additional ingredients, cornmeal quickly became a very tiresome food.

Apples were pervasive, and if out of season, dried apples were always available. They were inexpensive and easy to carry and didn't take up any space to speak of, at least as long as the package didn't get wet. More than one pioneer journal entry recounts the tremendous expansive qualities of dried apples when caught unprotected in a rain storm. A box exposed on a rainy day resulted in a bounty of moist apples that were quickly added to every food imaginable. No doubt this led to some interesting combinations.

Perhaps this is how the notion of Apple-Corn Loaf came about. Whatever the reason, it had an unusual but delicious outcome. Our modern-day recipe calls for at least one egg to bind the ingredients.

Peel and dice the apple. Place in a bowl and mix sugar with pple until the apple is covered. Leave for 15 minutes to let juice form. If afraid of discoloration, add ½ teaspoon lemon juice. In a separate bowl, mix cornmeal, flour, salt, and baking powder. Add egg, milk, and butter, stirring until blended. Pour into a well-greased 4 x 6-inch loaf pan and cover top with apples. Bake in a preheated oven. It is done when an inserted toothpick comes out dry. Turn out of pan and cool on a wire rack.

The fresh apple offers a nice crunch to the corn bread. Just a bit of butter on a warm slice makes a wonderful addition to dinner.

VARIATIONS

⌁ If you prefer softer apples, turn the

(continued on following page)

diced apple and sugar in a sauce pan with a tablespoon of butter, and cook on low heat until soft. Add to the recipe and bake normally.

~ Other fruits work well. Pears and apricots are especially good.

~ For an apple pie flavor, add 1 teaspoon cinnamon to the apples while they are standing.

Butterscotch Biscuits

BAKING TIME: *25 minutes*
OVEN TEMPERATURE: *375 degrees*

Biscuits:
 3 cups all-purpose flour
 2 teaspoons baking powder
 ¼ cup granulated sugar
 ½ teaspoon salt
 4 tablespoons butter
 2 eggs, beaten
 ½ cup milk
Filling:
 4 tablespoons butter, melted
 4 tablespoons corn syrup
 1 cup brown sugar

Combine all dry ingredients, and blend well. Cut in butter. Add eggs and milk to the dry mix, and blend until combined. If the mixture is too wet, add a bit more

(continued on following page)

There is a tendency to think of butterscotch as a separate ingredient flavoring candy or topping ice cream sundaes. In reality, it is a very simple mix of butter and brown sugar.

Butterscotch is easy to make, and this simplicity resulted in many butter and brown sugar treats in the Old West. The term butterscotch was not often used in the Old West, and few references list "butterscotch" as an ingredient, but the basic ingredients were employed in various dishes for flavor and variety. Although ranch cooks may not have had a name for it, butterscotch biscuits appeared in many Old West ranch houses.

CHUCK WAGON ACCESSORIES

Much like we do with automobiles, chuck wagon cooks accessorized wagons to suit needs and tastes. Hanging off the side of this land cruiser would be any number of barrels containing water, grains, and whatnot. Joining the barrels for dusty rides were pans, ropes, a coffee grinder, and tool boxes.

Since chuck wagons carried supplies for a month or more, space was precious. To expand storage, a hammock was strung beneath the wagon to hold campfire fuel. If wood wasn't available, the cook gathered cow or buffalo "prairie coal," let it dry, and used it like wood. This hammock, or "possum belly," could carry anything, as long as one didn't mind it being mixed with dried manure. Few items other than wood were ever volunteered for this duty.

flour. The fewer strokes the better. Spread out dough with flour-covered hands on a lightly floured area about ½–1 inch thick.

Mix the filling ingredients. Spread a thin layer over the biscuit dough and the remaining into a baking dish. Roll the biscuit dough up as a jelly roll. Slice into 1-inch pieces and place the pieces into the wet baking dish (stick the biscuit pieces together as a simple puzzle). Bake uncovered in a preheated oven. When done, turn out immediately. Be careful, the butterscotch is *very* hot. The easiest way is to place a plate over the baking pan, turning the whole combination upside down, away from your body. Lift the baking dish off of your masterpiece and let it set up for a few minutes.

Serve warm, out of the oven and into the stomach. It really doesn't need anything else.

VARIATIONS

↬ Adding ¼ teaspoon cinnamon gives these biscuits a completely different and delicious character.

↬ Chopped walnuts are a nice touch. Sprinkle ¼ cup or more over the bottom of the baking dish before adding anything else.

Beaten Biscuits

BAKING TIME: *20–30 minutes*
OVEN TEMPERATURE: *350 degrees*

3 cups all-purpose flour
1 teaspoon granulated sugar
1 teaspoon salt
1 tablespoon butter or margarine
1 cup water, as needed

In a large bowl, mix flour, sugar, and salt. Cut in butter with fingers until the dough is coarse and mealy. Slowly add water to make a stiff dough. Turn out on floured board and knead until all is mixed well. Roll or pat out to about ½ inch thick, and beat with a mallet. When flat, fold over to make ½-inch-thick dough again, and beat some more. Repeat until elastic. Let the dough rise at least an hour, but better if prepared the day before and allowed to rise through the night. Then roll or pat out to ½ inch thick, and cut with a biscuit cutter or a large upside-down cup. Place on a greased cookie sheet, and let rise again for at least an hour. Bake in a pre-heated oven. Done when golden brown.

Serve warm, fresh out of the oven.

Although often thought of as Southern, Beaten Biscuits are the perfect solution to anyone facing the disaster of inactive sourdough starter or an empty baking soda container. Without a leavening agent to create air, air had to be developed in the flour itself, so the dough was literally beaten with a mallet for fifteen to twenty minutes. This strengthened the dough and trapped enough air to lighten it.

Due to the intensive labor involved, Beaten Biscuits were not high on the list of popular options for baker, but on the open range this was often the only way to get biscuits with a palatable texture. Chuck wagon cooks would recruit a gullible new cowhand for help, sitting him somewhere close by with a mallet and not letting him mosey off until the dough was just the right consistency.

Beaten Biscuits are very heavy biscuits, almost a cross between hardtack and bread. Don't expect an airy, fluffy product.

This recipe can also serve as a wonderful introduction into baking for children. Just be careful where the mallet lands.

Crackling Bread

BAKING TIME: *20–30 minutes*
OVEN TEMPERATURE: *400 degrees*

> *1 cup finely diced salt pork*
> *1 cup cornmeal*
> *1 cup all-purpose flour*
> *2 teaspoons baking soda*
> *2 eggs, beaten*
> *1 cup buttermilk*

True Crackling Bread is almost impossible to find, but just a century ago it was one of the most popular special breads available. Cracklings were originally the crisp bits of pork remaining after rendering lard. They were tasty and crunchy and were used in a number of dishes, but none as grand as this bread.

Although its history is obscure, Crackling Bread is believed to have been developed in the South. It moved west with the pioneers to be enjoyed by all residents. Even Native Americans added cracklings to their versions of corn dodger and bean-corn breads. Ranch hands also considered it a great treat, and Old West hotels included it on menus. Obtaining cracklings wasn't a problem since lard was used as often as today's butter and shortening, but as the use of lard fell off, cracklings became scarce.

To make the bread today, diced salt pork is substituted. The flavor is close and certainly worth the delicious visit to the past.

Brown pork in a skillet. Pull out "cracklings" and set aside. Reserve drippings. In a separate bowl, mix cornmeal, flour, and baking soda. Pour in eggs and buttermilk, alternating and mixing constantly. Fold in cracklings, with a tablespoon of the remaining skillet fat, if desired. Spread batter in a well-greased roasting pan to about 1 inch thick. Bake in a preheated oven. Done when it springs back to the touch. Remove and cool. Slice as you would corn bread.

Delicious served warm, with sweet butter.

VARIATION

If a sweeter taste is desired, add 2 tablespoons of granulated sugar to the dry ingredients.

English Soda Muffins

SKILLET TIME: *5 minutes per side*
SKILLET TEMPERATURE: *medium*

2 cups all-purpose flour
2 teaspoons granulated sugar
2 teaspoons baking soda
½ teaspoon salt
1 cup buttermilk
2 eggs, beaten
1 tablespoon vegetable oil or butter

Mix flour, sugar, soda, and salt in a large bowl. Pour buttermilk and eggs into the bowl, alternating each, and mix lightly. Prepare a large skillet with vegetable oil or butter, and place well-greased muffin rings in the skillet. With wet hands, form a golf ball–sized piece of dough and sprinkle with cornmeal. Place directly into the rings and flatten if necessary. If the dough is very stiff, rings may not be necessary. Cook until light brown, and turn. When done, place on a wire rack to cool.

English muffin critics claim the only way to eat one is to split it with a fork, never to slice it with a knife. This way more ridges appear to hold butter or jam.

VARIATION
↪ There is hardly a better vessel for raisins. Mix ½ cup into the batter.

Surprisingly, it is unclear where English muffins originated. Recipes were found on both sides of the ocean at about the same time. The American version generally used sourdough starter, whereas the English version used baking soda. (Refer to page 63 for a sourdough English muffin variety.) Both muffin recipes are very airy, meaning the bread has numerous pockets of air to make the distinctive English muffin texture, better in texture and flavor than the supermarket version.

In the Old West, English muffins were baked on a skillet. The heavy cast-iron skillet was well greased with lard, and a round ring made out of an old tin can was placed directly on top. The batter was then poured or pressed into the ring and baked over an open fire.

Here is the baking soda version of the recipe. Muffin rings can be purchased at most cooking supply stores, or you can make your own by using well-washed tuna-fish cans with the tops and bottoms removed.

Hunkydummy

BAKING TIME: *10–15 minutes*
OVEN TEMPERATURE: *400 degrees*

> *2 cups all-purpose flour*
> *2 teaspoons baking powder*
> *½ teaspoon salt*
> *¼ cup solid shortening*
> *1 cup milk*
> *½ cup raisins*

Biscuits came with many names, but when something special was added, such as raisins, they became known as Hunkydummy. The origin of the name is anybody's guess.

Like other biscuits, if Hunkydummy didn't turn out just right, range cowboys would make up names that reflected their thoughts on product quality. "Sinkers," "hot rocks," or "bullets" were common labels. Often a flashy story would accompany this creative endeavor. For example, an experienced cowpoke might tell of biscuits that were so bad, they were thrown into the river and sank like rocks. That wasn't the half of it. A few minutes later a fish floated to the surface—its mouth shattered from trying to eat it!

It's easy to envision the cook's reception to this tall tale: Biscuits might not be on the menu for awhile.

Blend the flour, baking powder, and salt. Cut shortening into the dry mix with a pastry blender or use two knives. Keep at it until it has the texture of tiny pebbles. Pour in all the milk and raisins, and stir until stiff. Turn out the whole batch on a lightly floured area, and sprinkle the top with a bit of the flour lying around. Knead lightly, squeezing and compressing about 8–10 times. Now pat out about ½ inch thick. Cut the biscuits with a round cookie cutter or the end of an empty jar the size of your choice. Place on a lightly greased sheet, and bake in a preheated oven until golden brown. Serve piping hot.

Serve immediately, the hotter the better. Keeps fresh for about two days.

VARIATIONS
↪ Raisins can be deleted easily, and other goodies added: grated cheese, orange bits,

(continued on following page)

cinnamon, etc. Use your imagination.

༂ Super-rich biscuits can be fashioned by using cold butter instead of shortening. Assemble the same way.

༂ Serve with a dispenser of honey, a nice alternative to butter.

Chuckwagon, ca. 1900.

Indian Flat Bread

BAKING TIME: *moments*
ROCK TEMPERATURE: *hot*

> 3 cups blue corn
> 2 cups water
> ash (a few tablespoons, as needed)

*T*his is the traditional Indian bread. The Hopi called it piki, *the Zuni,* hewe, *and the Tewa,* mowa. *It has as many names as there are tribes.*

Whatever its name, preparation is basically the same. However, it is rarely recreated in modern kitchens, for a number of reasons. The first problem is that it requires a very adept hand to make correctly and hundreds of attempts to gain the necessary skill to get the proper thickness. The second difficulty is the need for a very hot, flat stone to grill the bread. This two-foot-wide, four-inch-thick, ten-pound flat rock is not a typical kitchen accessory.

Ingredients vary little from tribe to tribe. Cornmeal batter (usually blue corn) and strained ash water (from juniper trees, corn cobs, or cedar wood) were all that was required.

Finely grind dried blue corn, preferably on a very level grinding stone. Mix 1 cup of water with the cornmeal. Place a few tablespoons of ash in a second cup of water and stir. Strain the ash water through a batch of tightly woven grasses to catch the ash. Mix the strained water with the cornmeal and blend.

In a separate area, light a fire and allow it to burn down to hot coals. Elevate your rock about 6–8 inches above the fire and heat to about 700 degrees. You'll know the rock is hot enough when watermelon seeds brown on the stone.

Dip four unburned fingers (assuming this is your first attempt) into the mix and quickly swipe the blend over the hot stone, first up and down, then back and forth. Let it grill for a few seconds, then remove and roll it as you would a tamale.

Roll up the thin bread and serve in a basket.

Oatmeal-Apricot Loaf

BAKING TIME: *45–55 minutes*
OVEN TEMPERATURE: *350 degrees*

2 cups all-purpose flour
1 cup rolled oats
½ cup granulated sugar
2 teaspoons baking powder
1 teaspoon salt
1 cup milk
1 egg, beaten
½ cup butter or margarine, melted
½ cup dried apricots

Combine flour, oats, sugar, baking powder, and salt. Stir well. In a separate bowl, combine milk, egg, and melted butter. Stir wet ingredients into the dry ingredients. Do so gently; do not overmix. Chop apricots and mix in. Pour into well-greased loaf pan and bake in preheated oven until golden brown. Test by sticking a toothpick into loaf. It's done when it comes out dry. Cool on wire rack.

Cool and slice. Great when served with or without a bit of butter. For the kids, try the slices as a peanut butter sandwich.

VARIATIONS
∽ The recipe will accept virtually any kind of nut desired. About ½ cup will work well.
∽ Dried mixed fruit can be substituted for apricots, or try ½ cup raisins with the mix.

What were cattle-driving cowboys and pioneers doing with apricots? By the nineteenth century, food technology had come far enough to make packaged dried fruit available. However, cost was an issue. If a cowboy were lucky enough to hire on with a generous wealthy rancher, dried fruit was included on chuck wagon inventories. Dried fruit allowed "Cookie" to create a variety of special treats for tired cowboys. It was used in numerous quick breads and biscuits. Wagon trains, even more limited in space, usually carried dried fruits during the first months of the long trip when weight and space weren't a concern yet. As they approached the mountainous terrain, dried fruits were often the first to be left behind. The wildlife must have eaten very well.

But, until then, everyone enjoyed a variety of fruit quick breads and puddings.

Old Range Biscuits

Although many of the romantic memories of cattle drives focus on the sweet aroma of sourdough, sourdough breads took time and patience to make. Biscuits assembled with baking soda or baking powder, however, could be on a cowboy's tin serving plate in thirty minutes, start to finish. So, if the chuck wagon cook was in a particularly foul humor, or just ran short of time, he'd make quick biscuits.

Some chuck wagon "cookies" became so adept at quick biscuits that they didn't even dirty any pans when assembling the mix. They would simply tear open the sack of flour, make a deep well, and blend in the baking soda, salt, and lard. After they added a little water to the fresh biscuit dough, it was ready for the dutch oven.

One of perhaps a hundred ways to fix quick biscuits, these Old Range Biscuits are virtually fail-safe. They are simple, tasty, and quick.

Mercifully, in this recipe butter is substituted for lard. Also, this is one of the few quick breads that improve with mild kneading. Do so carefully, and don't add too much flour, which will result in dry biscuits.

BAKING TIME: *12 minutes*
OVEN TEMPERATURE: *400 degrees*

> 2 cups all-purpose flour
> 1 teaspoon salt
> 1½ teaspoons baking soda
> 1 tablespoon granulated sugar
> 3 tablespoons butter or margarine
> 1 cup buttermilk

Combine dry ingredients. Stir to mix. Melt butter, and slowly add butter and buttermilk to the dry mix, blending thoroughly. Knead lightly, for about 2 minutes. A bit of vegetable oil on your hands will help release the sticky dough. Pat out the dough on a lightly floured board to about ½ inch thick, and cut to a convenient size with a cookie cutter or the open end of a round cup. Place on a well-greased cookie sheet and bake immediately in a preheated oven until golden brown. Cool on a wire rack.

If possible, serve within an hour of baking. Best if eaten within a day.

Pumpkin Loaf

BAKING TIME: *50 minutes*
OVEN TEMPERATURE: *350 degrees*

  2 cups all-purpose flour
  2 teapoons baking powder
  ¾ cup granulated sugar
  1 teaspoon cinnamon
  ¼ teaspoon powdered cloves
  ¼ teaspoon allspice
  2 eggs, beaten
  1 cup milk
  ½ cup canned pumpkin

In one bowl, mix flour, baking soda, sugar, and spices. Blend well. In a separate bowl combine eggs, milk, and canned pumpkin. Stir until blended. Mix dry ingredients into egg mix. Pour into well-greased 7-inch loaf pan and bake in pre-heated oven. The bread is done when it is lightly browned and springs back to the touch, or when a toothpick inserted into loaf comes out dry. Turn out immediately on a cooling rack.

Hot or cold, a slice will satisfy most longings for sweets. For a dessert, slice thick and top with fresh whipped cream.

VARIATIONS
↪ Add ½ cup nuts with wet ingredients.
↪ For a tang, add 1 teaspoon orange bits and ½ cup raisins.

Although pumpkin is usually synonymous with Halloween celebrations and Thanksgiving, it was grown on this continent long before the arrival of Europeans. Native Americans used the squash as a vegetable, a base for soup, and an addition to breads and puddings.

For pioneers, wagon trains would hopefully be winding up the long summer passage to the West at the beginning of pumpkin season. With supplies low, and pioneers' taste buds longing for different flavors, pumpkin was a real treat to add to biscuits, pies, and breads. Even without the fall season for fresh pumpkin, dried pumpkin was occasionally available to pioneers at provision stops. For those who could afford the room in tightly packed wagons, sharing pumpkin was a wonderful way to make new friends.

Today we have canned pumpkin every bit as good as fresh. Because storage room in the kitchen isn't a significant problem, don't wait until the winter holidays to make this easy, tasty loaf. It is similar in flavor and coarse texture to those made for the last one hundred years.

Rice Loaf

Rice wasn't widely used in the Old West until late in the history of range cooking. It wasn't that it didn't taste great; it's just that few knew how to prepare it. Many entertaining stories tell of cooks placing two or three handfuls in a small pot and the resulting expansive mess flowing all over the campfire. When cooks finally cracked the code on portion control, they blended rice with many other ingredients. The "swamp seed," as it was termed, was versatile and tasty.

This is an example of one of its many uses. It's also one of the nicest-textured loaves in the entire quick bread family.

BAKING TIME: *15–18 minutes*
OVEN TEMPERATURE: *400 degrees*

1 egg, beaten
1¼ cups milk
2 tablespoons butter, melted
1¼ cups cooked rice
1 tablespoon baking powder
1 tablespoon granulated sugar
¼ teaspoon salt
2 cups all-purpose flour

Blend egg, milk, and melted butter. Stir in rice until well mixed. In a separate bowl, blend baking powder, sugar, salt, and flour. Add the dry ingredients to the wet ingredients. Stir just enough to blend, about 20 seconds at the most. There will be lumps, but that's OK. Pour into buttered 7-inch loaf pan, or use muffin cups and fill to two-thirds full. Place into preheated oven and bake until tops are rounded, cracked, and brown, about 15–18 minutes. Cool on wire rack.

Serve hot, cold, or in between; they work well at any temperature.

VARIATIONS
∽ Add ½ cup raisins with the rice.
∽ For a "ricier" taste, add ½ cup of rice flour and reduce the all-purpose by the same amount.

(continued on following page)

⸙ A teaspoon of orange bits added with the dry ingredients, or a tablespoon of orange marmalade added with the wet ingredients, creates a nice zip.

Spider Bread

BAKING TIME: *25 minutes*
OVEN TEMPERATURE: *350 degrees*

> *1 cup cornmeal*
> *1 cup all-purpose flour*
> *1 teaspoon baking soda*
> *½ teaspoon salt*
> *¼ cup granulated sugar*
> *1 cup buttermilk*
> *1 egg, beaten*
> *2 tablespoons butter or*
>   *margarine, melted*

In a large mixing bowl, blend all the dry ingredients. Add buttermilk, egg, and melted butter. Lightly blend until just mixed. Pour into well-greased 9-inch or 10-inch frying pan and bake. If no frying pan is available, use a large cake pan. Spider bread is done when an inserted toothpick comes out cleanly.

When served piping hot with butter melting, Spider Bread just can't be beat. Slice into pie-shaped wedges.

(continued on following page)

Also called skillet corn bread, *Spider Bread has been around for at least two hundred years. Spider Bread was cooked in an open frying pan. The heavy cast-iron skillet was designed to stand on three "spiderlike" legs over hot coals. The hot fire could bake the bread in fifteen minutes, perfect for chuck wagon or wagon train cooks on the move. Since skillet breads baked so quickly, their texture left something to be desired, but this mattered little to hungry trail riders.*

Our updated recipe bakes Spider Bread in the oven for a finer, more evenly textured dish, but it maintains the look of the Old West variety and is a hearty corn food you won't soon forget.

∽ For a bit of extra sweetness, add 2 tea-spoons honey with melted butter.

∽ A stronger dessertlike flavor is possible by pouring honey over the bread before serving.

Western Ginger Loaf

BAKING TIME: *7–10 minutes*
OVEN TEMPERATURE: *350 degrees*

> *½ cup butter or margarine*
> *½ cup granulated sugar*
> *1 egg, beaten*
> *2 cups all-purpose flour*
> *2 teaspoons baking powder*
> *½ teaspoon salt*
> *1 teaspoon ginger*
> *1 teaspoon vanilla*
> *½ cup molasses*
> *1 cup milk*

Fresh ginger was out of the question for most pioneers on the move, but dried ginger was readily available and inexpensive.

Many original European recipes for baked goods called for mixtures of pepper, cloves, cinnamon, saffron, mace, and ginger—all in one recipe. When they moved to the colonies, settlers streamlined baking and cooking by using only a few spices in each dish. This simplification was carried into the Old West, where cooks carted only a few spices at most. The most popular were cinnamon and ginger.

Gingerbread was a natural development of scarce spices. More a cake than bread, it had a sharp, distinctive taste and was easily prepared. Virtually all journals from early settlers make reference to a form of gingerbread.

Beat butter and sugar together until light. Beat in egg. In a separate bowl, blend flour, baking powder, salt, and ginger. Mix vanilla, molasses, and milk in another bowl. Add to dry mix and stir; do not overbeat. Butter a 10-inch springform pan. Spread mixture, and bake in preheated oven until brown. Cut into squares while still hot, and put squares onto cooling rack.

(continued on following page)

Warm or cold, a slice of gingerbread topped with powdered sugar is a real treat.

VARIATIONS
∽ Do as the pioneers did and serve the gingerbread with a jelly or jam spread.
∽ Slice thin and cover with cream cheese.
∽ Raisins offer a distinctive taste in gingerbread; try ½ cup.

Whole Wheat–Date Loaf

BAKING TIME: *15–20 minutes*
OVEN TEMPERATURE: *400 degrees*

> *1 cup all-purpose flour*
> *1½ cups whole wheat flour*
> *2 teaspoons baking powder*
> *½ teaspoon salt*
> *4 tablespoons brown sugar*
> *1¼ cups milk or buttermilk*
> *1 egg, beaten*
> *¼ cup butter or margarine, melted*
> *¾ cup chopped dates*

Blend all dry ingredients in a large bowl—flours, baking powder, salt, and brown sugar. In another bowl, mix milk, egg, and butter; after they are well mixed, add dates and pour the batter into the dry ingredients. Stir to blend, but not for more than 20 seconds. The mix will be lumpy,

(continued on following page)

This simple mix is well over one hundred years old. It is unusual because it calls for the mix to be spread thinly in the bottom of a large pan. This makes for a drier bread, but it keeps well and is easy to eat on the go. For a moist loaf, use a buttered 8-inch loaf or cake pan and bake for forty-five minutes.

*M*ost of the flour milled in the early-nineteenth-century Old West was whole wheat. It took many extra steps to mill pure white flour, usually making it too expensive for common use. As a direct result, kitchen sifters became an item of self-defense for range cooks. Sifters were designed not only to assist making light and fluffy goods, but more importantly, to sift each and every pound of whole wheat flour in order to separate stones, dirt chunks, and other miscellaneous treats blended in the sacks. Packaging standards were well short of today's expectations.

This loaf recipe is representative of commonly available whole wheat flour and has a very strong whole wheat taste and texture.

END OF THE DRIVE

Rewards awaited at the ends of long drives, which lasted three months or more. The twenty-five dollars per month cowboys were paid bought all the luxuries they could possibly desire: a comfortable bed, a shot of whiskey, and a meal not prepared by the chuck wagon cook.

Destination towns were serviced by railroads. Since most trains heading west to pick up cattle were virtually empty, there was plenty of room on board for delivery of ingredients not available on the range. Fruits, grains, and the like were brought in for shops that ruthlessly marked up the prices.

Cowboys fresh off the range were willing to pay. Dodge City's Wright, Beverly and Company did a thousand dollars a day in general goods with the arrival of a herd for market. This is when boots were three dollars a pair.

but that's OK. Place into well-buttered 7-inch loaf pan, or use a muffin pan and fill to two-thirds full. Bake until lightly browned. Cool on wire rack.

Especially good served warm with melted butter or in a dish with honey.

VARIATION

∽ If dates aren't to your taste, try raisins or eliminate fruit all together.

∽ These are also great with ½ cup chopped walnuts, added at the same time as the dates.

∽ For a different flavor, delete the dates and substitute roasted, shelled pumpkin seeds.

∽ Use buttermilk instead of regular milk.

Gems: Yesteryear's Muffins

ONE CAN RARELY FIND GEMS MENTIONED ANYWHERE TODAY, BUT just one hundred years ago they were so wildly popular that few bakers' kitchens were ever without a special pan to fix the delightful treat. As an indication of their true value, some pioneers risked the extra weight to include a favorite gem pan among provisions taken West. For those unable or unwilling to chance the additional burden, shipping companies ensured a broad selection in West Coast cities upon the pioneers' arrival. Thousands considered the forty or sixty cents well worth the expense to have gems back on their table.

The history of gems is unclear, but in the nineteenth century manufacturers cast special baking pans just for gems. They looked very similar to muffin pans, but came in a much wider variety of shapes and sizes. Nineteenth-century gem pan castings were exquisite compared to today's reproductions. Many pans were representative of the finest ironwork of the time, and they baked superbly, with an even heat only a quality casting could generate. Although no baker worth flour would ever have allowed it, some pans were so attractive that soap manufacturers used them as molds for specialty products.

Preparing a new gem pan was relatively simple. A user filled each cup with a mix of water and ash, then placed the pan into high heat to "cure." A well-stoked wood stove worked superbly. After curing, the pans were washed once again with ash and well greased before the first use. Early gem bakers used only cast-iron gem pans and assembled the treat with whole wheat or graham flour. No white flour was allowed.

By the early 1900s, gems fell out of favor, and it became almost impossible to determine just what constituted a real one any longer. Popover pans, roll pans, and such were now all labeled gem pans.

Understandably, most of today's kitchens are without cast-iron pans of any sort, but a credible job can be accomplished with the heaviest muffin pan you can find. If yours are light aluminum, double them up by inserting the second pan into the first—not ideal, but it helps.

Assembly is much like that for muffins: the less blended, the better. The flour used is much heavier than you may be used to, so expect a denser product. Standard whole wheat flour found on grocery shelves works nicely. As you develop a taste for the unique qualities of gems, you might turn to graham flour, which can be found at many health food stores. Cornmeal is called for in one recipe, creating an even denser gem. Cornmeal has little gluten, the magic glue allowing bread to rise. To lighten the texture of the Corn Gem for modern preferences, white flour is added.

Most gems are made as a batter, so kneading is impossible. The best way to handle the wet dough is to use a large tablespoon and drop a few ounces of raw gem batter into the selected baking medium. A hint from an old hand at panning gems is to dip the tablespoon into cold water before each use. Each gem mix will slide off the spoon "as quick as you please."

Finally, gems are baked in a very hot oven, at least four hundred degrees. Check each recipe for recommendations.

Chuckwagon and camp.

Graham Gems

BAKING TIME: *20 minutes*

OVEN TEMPERATURE: *400 degrees*

> *½ cup granulated sugar*
> *4 tablespoons butter or margarine*
> *2 eggs*
> *2 cups graham flour*
> *1 cup all-purpose flour*
> *1 teaspoon baking soda*
> *1½ cups buttermilk*

Mix sugar and butter together with a fork until well blended. Add whole eggs and mix well. In a separate bowl, mix flours and baking soda, and add to butter mix, alternating with a bit of milk until all is blended. Do not overwork. Spoon into well-greased gem or muffin pan to two-thirds full. Bake immediately. When lightly browned, remove from oven and turn out on cooling rack.

Interestingly enough, the original 1866 recipe called for "a good sized piece of lard." As best can be determined, this meant about one-half cup. Here, we reduce it to four tablespoons to cut fat to reasonable levels. If no buttermilk is available, substitute whole milk and change the baking soda to baking powder. The recipe makes two dozen.

Cornmeal Gems

Cornmeal is very difficult to make into light fluffy gems without the addition of some flour. The Old West bakers didn't bother, and you needn't either if a heavier product suits your fancy. Just delete the white flour and add another cup of cornmeal.

BAKING TIME: *15–20 minutes*
OVEN TEMPERATURE: *400 degrees*

> *1 cup cornmeal*
> *½ teaspoon salt*
> *2 tablespoons granulated sugar*
> *1 cup boiling water*
> *2 eggs*
> *1 cup milk*
> *1½ cups all-purpose flour*
> *2 teaspoons baking powder*

Mix cornmeal, salt, and sugar in a large bowl. Add boiling water and stir briskly. When cooled slightly (so eggs won't cook), add both eggs and milk, and mix. Now stir in flour and baking powder. Mix should appear to be a very thick batter. If not thick enough, add more flour until it reaches the consistency of thin mashed potatoes. Do not overwork. Spoon into well-greased gem or muffin pan to two-thirds full. Bake immediately. When golden brown, remove from oven and turn out on cooling rack.

Buttermilk Gems

BAKING TIME: *20 minutes*

OVEN TEMPERATURE: *400 degrees*

> *1 cup cornmeal*
> *2 cups white or graham flour*
> *½ cup granulated sugar*
> *1 teaspoon baking soda*
> *½ teaspoon salt*
> *2 cups buttermilk*
> *1 egg*

Mix dry ingredients. Add half the milk, then the egg, and blend. Add remaining buttermilk and stir until blended. Do not overwork. Spoon into well-greased gem or muffin pan. Bake immediately. When golden brown, remove from oven and turn out on cooling rack.

The recipe makes two dozen.

Buttermilk Gems are probably closer to biscuits than gems, but because they were baked in gem pans for easy eating, they qualify. The lighter texture and flavor reflects the age of the recipe. It came out of a Southwest cookbook at the turn of the century. It was just one of many recipes demonstrating the changing tastes of the new population.

Corn Bread: *"Giver of Life"*

I F ANY ONE FOOD ITEM WAS CONSIDERED A STAPLE IN THE OLD WEST, it was corn. It grew with relative ease and was cultivated throughout the area. However, corn didn't enjoy the best reputation among European descendants working and making their way through this territory. Because it was used in virtually everything, most new settlers quickly tired of it and corn became the butt of many jokes. This was most likely because they didn't know how to prepare, or appreciate, its variety.

Native Americans used corn for as long as their history tells. It grew in such abundance that it became a symbol of fertility and beneficence to virtually all tribes of the western United States. The Hopis alone had twenty varieties of corn, each with its own legends and beliefs. Native Americans attached ceremony to every stage of corn growth, including harvesting and meal preparation.

Most corn was shucked and roasted on hot coals or in an adobe oven. Dried, it could be stored for years. If the tribe had a particularly good harvest, they placed at least an extra year's supply in storage for bad growing seasons.

Corn kernels have little gluten to bind the mix so it can rise, so most Indian breads and dumplinglike products were flat and dense. When new settlers introduced wheat to western tribes, they found mixing corn flour with wheat flour produced softer baked goods. Even a mash of wheat and corn buried in hot coals was strong enough to rise and create a chewy and evenly textured bread.

The following recipes represent some of the most popular of the era. They blend and bake a bit differently than you may be used to, but they are as authentic as possible. So step back one hundred and fifty years and enjoy the cornmeal baked goods of yesteryear.

Pictured from top are Old Range Biscuits (page 20) and corn bread (see Corn Muffins Variations, page 34).

Corn Muffins

ometimes misnamed gems, muffins were baked in deeper pans and were not quite as breadlike as gems. Muffins graduated from being cooked in a utensil called muffin rings to special baking pans. Muffin rings were hooplike accessories placed directly on a hot stove or the bottom of a skillet. Batter was then poured into them. The rings did not prove to be as popular with muffin consumers as molds of the same period. However, their demise as holders of raw muffin batter was not in vain, for they remain a valuable kitchen accessory to make popular English muffins or fried eggs.

The muffin molds of the nineteenth century turned out to be an extremely efficient product. They baked their contents thoroughly and very evenly. We would envy such a casting quality today.

This recipe was designed primarily for ranch house bakers and western hotel restaurants where milk, butter, and eggs were plentiful. Those cooking out of the back of a chuck wagon or covered wagon had a difficult time preparing good muffins.

BAKING TIME: *15 minutes*
OVEN TEMPERATURE: *400 degrees*

> ½ cup butter or margarine
> ¾ cup granulated sugar
> 2 eggs
> 2 cups all-purpose flour
> 1 cup cornmeal
> 2 teaspoons baking powder
> ½ teaspoon salt
> 1 cup milk

Cream the butter and sugar until light and fluffy. Add the eggs and blend. Do not overbeat. In a separate bowl, mix flour, cornmeal, baking powder, and salt. Alternate adding dry mixture and milk to the butter mixture until just mixed. Pour into lightly greased muffin pans to about two-thirds full. Bake in a preheated oven. Tops will spring back when done. Turn out immediately.

They hold their fresh flavor for only a few days, so serve immediately. Honey works wonders on hot corn muffins.

VARIATIONS
~ To make corn bread, pour batter into greased 9 x 9-inch baking pan and bake for 25 minutes at 400 degrees.
~ Add ½ cup shredded cheese right after mixing the eggs. Mild cheddar works well.

Corn Dodgers

BAKING TIME: *10–15 minutes*
OVEN TEMPERATURE: *400 degrees*

2 cups yellow cornmeal
2 tablespoons butter or margarine
½ teaspoon salt
1 tablespoon granulated sugar
2 cups milk
1 teaspoon baking powder

Cook cornmeal in a saucepan with butter, salt, sugar, and milk until the mixture comes to a boil. Turn off heat, cover, and let stand 5 minutes. Add baking powder. Spoon the mix onto the greased cookie sheet in heaping tablespoon-sized balls, and bake in a hot oven. Done when slightly brown around the edges.

Designed as a handy way to eat corn bread, they can be cut laterally and filled with a honey butter for an afternoon treat. They don't keep long, so the sooner consumed the better.

VARIATIONS
∽ To make a spicy version, add 2 tablespoons (more if your taste buds can stand it) of chopped jalapeños to the mix.
∽ Add ¼ cup of shredded sharp cheddar cheese helps with or without the peppers.

Corn bread was one of the most popular American staples, maybe not always because of its flavor, but because of its cost. Corn kernels were relatively inexpensive and easily shipped. Cornmeal was also one of the core supplies aboard wagons heading west. With it, one of the easiest quick breads took shape, Corn Dodgers. There must be a colorful story attached to the name, but it has been lost in history. What was unusual about Corn Dodgers was their size. Because they were designed for quick snacking in an era of few utensils, they were made in round patties about three inches across and one inch thick. This was a perfect size for trail cooks and riders with no extra hands. This recipe update includes milk and butter, like Corn Dodgers made in prairie homes.

Like Johnnycakes, Corn Dodgers are a heavy corn bread, and this recipe is very authentic.

Fried Corn Bread

*C*huck wagon, wagon train, ranch house, and Native American cooks had one pressing issue in common: Food was such a valuable commodity that it was never thrown away, but recycled. A perfect example was in the use of corn products. Stale corn bread was as valuable as fresh. It crumbled easily for use in new loaves or was easily added to other dishes. If dipped in water and reheated, it even had a fighting chance to taste reasonably close to fresh.

Here is a wonderful departure from any of the usual solutions for corn bread a bit south of fresh. It was drawn from an old Native American recipe book and designed as a sweet dessert—a rare treat indeed. The recipe has been brought up to date using modern ingredients, but it doesn't lose any of its spark.

FRYING TIME: *quick*
FRYING TEMPERATURE: *medium*

Sauce:
    2 tablespoons butter or margarine
    1 tablespoon flour
    2 cups whipping cream
    salt and pepper to taste
Bread:
    2 tablespoons butter or margarine
    stale corn bread, 1 loaf

To make the sauce, melt butter in a skillet and add flour. Mix rapidly with a whisk until blended. Brown the mix, then pour cream into the same skillet. Boil until thick, about the consistency of thick gravy. Add salt and pepper to taste. Pour into a separate dish, and in the same skillet, melt an additional 2 tablespoons butter.

To make the Fried Corn Bread, slice the loaf of corn bread into 1-inch-thick pieces. Over medium heat, brown corn bread slices in butter. Place the bread on a plate and pour cream mixture over the top.

Serve hot; it won't keep.

VARIATIONS
∽ For a sweeter taste, add a tablespoon of honey to the cream after it is boiled down. Mix in well.
∽ Apple-Corn Loaf, page 10, works wonderfully as Fried Corn Bread.

STOVES

The earliest stoves we know of were built in the Middle Ages for palaces in central Europe. They were made of earthenware and eventually became objects of art because of ornate designs each maker positioned on their product. By the early 1700s, the scientists got into the act and began perfecting ways to cast these designs in iron, and the cast-iron stove was born.

The earliest stoves in America go back to the early eighteenth century. As more and more stoves were built, their cost decreased so much that almost anyone could afford to purchase one. By the nineteenth century, the designers once again had control, and stoves sported not only design, but color.

They also found ingenious ways to integrate the numerous flues and other draft control devices into their layout. However, the development of electrical and gas service into the home killed further advancement of the designs, and most were melted down as scrap during the war years.

Johnnycake

BAKING TIME: *15 minutes*
OVEN TEMPERATURE: *400 degrees*

3 cups cornmeal
1 teaspoon salt
2 cups boiling water

Add all ingredients together and stir, stir, stir. By hand, it may take up to 15 minutes to get the mix frothy. Even with a little assistance from an electric mixer, it will take about 5 minutes. The mixture should be pliable. Shape into cakes about 4 inches in diameter. Place on well-greased cookie sheet. If it is not pliable, pour into a baking pan. Place in a hot oven. It is done when an inserted toothpick comes out dry.

VARIATION
⌢ To bring to modern taste and texture, add ½ cup milk, 1 beaten egg, 1 cup flour, and 1 tablespoon granulated sugar; mix together.

There are any number of ideas where the name Johnnycake originated, some far more creative than others. The tale sounding most logical states that the name is a convolution of the Narraganset name for corn, "jaunny."

Johnnycake's popularity is undeniable. Virtually every recipe book of the nineteenth century includes a recipe for Johnnycake. Most are simple, straightforward mixes of corn bread. As time passed and cookbook writers became more creative, so did Johnnycakes. Some recipes include ingredients such as buttermilk and eggs, but these products were not generally available to the working population, whose simple mix contained cornmeal, salt, and water.

However, you can customize this basic recipe and create a number of wonderful possibilities. Here is an authentic Johnnycake. It may be a bit dry and lack the sweetness of today's bread, but you owe it to yourself to taste what made it to western tables a century ago. (For a modern version, use the Variation.)

Aromatic Sourdough Breads

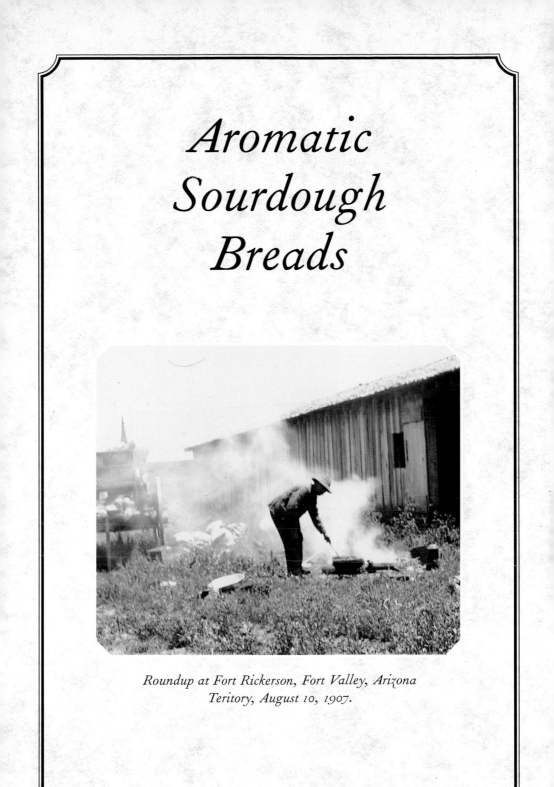

Roundup at Fort Rickerson, Fort Valley, Arizona Teritory, August 10, 1907.

Sourdough: The Best Friend of the Old West

BREAD NEEDS A LEAVENING AGENT TO RISE AND TO MAKE LIGHT and chewy loaves. This is usually accomplished by trapping carbon dioxide in the gluten, or protein, of the bread mass. Leavening can be chemical, like baking powder, or natural, like yeast. Today, many think of yeast as just a small packet of granulated, sweet-smelling material. In reality, it is a living organism.

Just a few decades ago, the only way to amass living yeast was by creating a "starter." Because starter takes time to develop its leavening ability, it sours and creates sourdough. Many credit the development of sourdough starter to western pioneers. It was carried by chuck wagon and wagon train cooks as a leavening agent for baked or pan-fried bread. Forty-niner loaves or San Francisco sourdough rounds are world famous. Because there were no refrigeration facilities in the Old West, fresh commercial yeast was out of the question. Instead, westerners used a mix that soured and ripened bread recipes, imparting a distinctive flavor.

However, if truth be told, the Old West was not responsible for the birth of sourdough. Sourdough started with the discovery of leavening agents by Egyptians about five thousand years ago. Through painstaking experimentation, Egyptians developed an active starter for a new, wildly popular beverage—beer. During the same millennium, an enterprising baker tried mixing a particularly hearty bacteria-laden starter sample with flour and water, creating the first leavened bread. A new industry was born. It was such a resounding success that the use of these wondrous sour yeast cultures spread rapidly through the Old World. They are still used throughout the Middle East and Europe as a principal leavening agent for their renowned breads.

Pictured, clockwise from upper left, are Whole Wheat Sourdough rolls (page 51), Classic Sourdough Bread (page 48), and Hornos Bread (page 52).

A word of caution before exploring sourdough: you will probably be witness to more failures than successes. If any characteristic stands out, true sourdough is consistently stubborn. Many expert bakers won't touch sourdough because of its temperamental nature. As a result, most store-bought sourdoughs have an added chemical that artificially induces sourdough taste; it is generally not real sourdough made with aged starter. We'll try it the honest way.

What Is Sourdough?

Sourdough is yeast fermented, or soured, in flour and liquid, breaking down the sugars to produce acids. These acids yield the pungent taste and smell.

Who Uses It?

Just a century ago, sourdough starter was still one of the most reliable sources for yeast cultures in the world. Old West residents from miners to ranchers made sourdough products daily, resulting in treats second to none.

Modern manufacturing has virtually eliminated the need for sourdough starter, but has not really duplicated the unique taste of real sourdough. Today, many European bakeries use sourdough cultures generations old in their breads and rolls. San Francisco was clever enough to pick up the marketing potential of the gold miner's staple, making a trademark of sourdough breads, rolls, muffins, cakes, and stuffing.

What Is a "Starter"?

Starter is the heart of the sourdough process. A small amount of starter added to a bowl of regular bread mix becomes the ringleader of change, quickly spreading its hosted, harmless bacteria among fresh ingredients. Imagine a video game with a mission to gobble up sugars and stuff, leaving a pungent, sharp taste behind. Starters do their work quickly and effectively.

Each starter has its own characteristic taste and smell. A starter created in San Francisco will not have the same flavor as one created in Omaha, but if cared for and well fed, it can live and grow indefinitely, no matter where it originates.

Many older starters are guarded by their owners as if they were a key to heaven. They are passed on generation to generation and rarely shared. Creating a starter presents an opportunity to create a legacy of your own, one that you may guard as zealously as you desire.

How Does All This Happen?

If a starter is not on hand, it should be made at least several days before baking. This allows proper fermentation and ensures the bread has that "sourdough tang."

The process consists of five steps:

1. Mix the starter.
2. Allow it to ferment.
3. Use it as a yeast mixture by adding additional ingredients.
4. Let this mix sour.
5. Pan it, and let it rise like a normal loaf of bread.

How Do I Get a Starter?

There are a few ways to get a starter. The easiest way is to acquire a sample from a friend. If you're fortunate enough to know someone with his or her own starter, convince that person of your undying loyalty or promise your firstborn for just a smidgin. That's all you need to make an infinite number of baked goods. If you lack a talented friend, a few varieties of starters are listed in this chapter. Others exist, and you're only limited by imagination. However, if you are just starting out, try the ones supplied.

Try It Now!

Because sourdough appears to have a will of its own, it remains a frightening prospect to many. Pitch out the apprehension. This isn't putting your ego or life savings on the line. It's a venture at directing a flamboyant, harmless bacteria that can resist horrendous amounts of abuse. Remember, pioneers used to make sourdough bread daily, and this was in the middle of the desert without so much as an oven. Think of it as returning to your roots.

Sourdough starter aromas are as different as the people preparing them. The captured taste and fragrance is largely based on luck. Each starter is like no other; it is a living organism with assorted bacteria working to make it uniquely yours. Failure at sourdoughs can become almost routine with even the most professional bakers, so don't expect the same resounding success you've experienced in other areas of baking. Even if you follow the recipes exactly as written, it's possible nothing will happen. The dough may not rise, and if it's truly stubborn, it may not even sour.

Most of these problems can be corrected. What can't be fixed is the appearance of strange colors in the mix. An orange or pink cast to the starter is a sign of bad bacteria. *Do not try to save it. Discard it immediately!* This is also true if the mix has a very unpleasant acrid odor. *Do not try to save it. Discard it immediately!* Be absolutely sure the utensils and containers used for the bad batch are cleaned before trying another. There is no sense going through the whole process only to grow another laboratory specimen.

How Is It Mixed?

Always use glass, plastic, or stainless steel for working and storing the mix. The high acid content of sourdough generates an undesirable flavor if it comes in contact with metal for any length of time.

Mixing and stirring a starter is just like mixing a normal loaf of bread except temperature is critical. It's particularly important the mix does not get too hot. Between 80 and 90 degrees is absolutely ideal. Some recipes call for 100 degrees, but rarely higher for fear of killing the starter. From this basic starter, we'll create a sponge.

Care and Feeding

Some very seasoned bakers making sourdoughs claim to have a bit of Old Western history baked into their breads because they use some original one-hundred-year-old starter in each and every loaf. This is not just a marketing ploy. As fermented yeast matures, it develops a richer taste impossible to achieve with young starters.

While this is all well and good, one of the major complaints with sourdoughs involves the care and feeding of the starter. It's possible to make sourdough bread as a one-shot deal and use all the starter in one mix, but by doing this, the flavor and smell of whatever unique bacteria you managed to capture is gone forever. The problem becomes one of keeping good bacteria healthy and not condemning it to an untimely demise.

Try the following:

- Store the starter in glass or plastic and in the refrigerator.
- Give it enough room in the container to grow about double in bulk. It rarely will in cold storage, but it's still warm when entering the dark, chilly reaches of the refrigerator shelf, so it will grow a bit before settling into dormancy.
- Starters need periodic feeding. Stirring in a dose of flour and liquid will do wonders, keeping the bacteria healthy and happy for at least two weeks. One cup of flour and one cup of liquid (usually water) are necessary to keep the starter from choking on its own by-products. This is also a good formula to replenish the starter used for baking.

Basic Starter

3 tablespoons plain yogurt
1 teaspoon sugar
1½ cups warm skim milk
1 cup all-purpose flour

Dissolve yogurt and sugar in warm milk. Cover bowl with plastic wrap and set aside in a warm place for 24 hours. By then, the starter should have a curd forming on top. When this happens, stir in flour and set aside in a warm, draft-free area for about 3–5 days, stirring at least twice a day. A pleasant sour aroma should be present, and the top of the mix should be covered with tiny bubbles.

Potato Starter

3 medium potatoes, peeled and boiled
2 cups all-purpose flour
2 cups warm water
2 tablespoons granulated sugar

Mash cooked potatoes thoroughly, and stir in half each of the flour, water, and sugar. Pour into a clean glass or stainless steel container and cover. Place in a warm area for 24 hours or until the mixture starts to bubble. It may take up to three days, so don't despair. Stir down at least every 12

(continued on following page)

hours. When mix has fermented (foaming and rising), pour into another container and add an additional cup of flour, water, and a tablespoon of sugar. Let it ferment another 24 hours; then it is ready to use. If desired, strain out any pieces of potato.

VARIATION

~ This recipe also works if cooked potatoes are grated, but they must be strained out before use in a bread recipe.

Honey Starter

2 cups warm water
1 package dry yeast
2 tablespoons honey
2 cups all-purpose flour

Water should be at least baby-bottle warm (warm when applied to the inside of the wrist). Add yeast and honey. When dissolved, stir in flour. Since this is activating live yeast from the packet, ensure that the temperature of the starter does not exceed 110 degrees or you'll kill the yeast. Place in a warm spot for 24–48 hours. It should start fermenting almost immediately. Let it rise and fall a few times to permit a souring process to develop. Stir down at least every 12 hours.

HONEY DOINGS

Although there may be some disagreement as to when honeybees made their first appearance in North America, they inarguably produced a sweetener treasured by both pioneers and Native Americans.

In early days it was said that for Native Americans the mere appearance of honeybees indicated the white man was within seventy-five to one hundred miles of their encampment.

Honey was easily extracted by soaking the comb in water. An interesting by-product was mead. Because honey was virtually all sugar, it fermented with a vengeance and formed a mild liquor within days.

For pioneers, honey presented a wonderful departure from sorghum. Honey had a wholesomeness about it; it took less to sweeten, so everything wasn't overwhelmed by the flavor.

KEEPING IT WARM

Prized by both cook and cowboy, the cherished starter found in wagon sourdough barrels was protected like a newborn baby. Starter was a necessity for a scrumptious variety of breads. To keep it fermenting, the batter had to be replenished and kept warm. At the ranch house, this was a relatively easy task accomplished by storing it behind a constantly stoked stove. On the trail, it presented a bit of a problem. During the day, the sun provided all the temperature control a keeper of the barrel could ask for. However, during a cool evening, it was necessary to move the barrel back and forth in front of the campfire to keep it at just the right temperature. As an easier alternative, it was not unusual for the cook to wrap the barrel in a blanket and tuck it into his bed, sharing his body heat with the precious batter.

Classic Sourdough Bread

BAKING TIME: *30–35 minutes*
OVEN TEMPERATURE: *375 degrees*

Sponge:
  1½ cups warm water
  1 teaspoon granulated sugar
  1 cup sourdough starter
  2 cups all-purpose or bread flour
Bread:
  3 cups bread flour
  2 teaspoons salt

Mix sponge ingredients. Stir well, place in a nonmetal bowl, and cover with plastic wrap. Set aside until mix is bubbly, about 8–12 hours.

To make bread, add flour and salt to fermenting sponge. Knead dough for about 10 minutes until elastic, or until the dough bounces back when poked. Let rise in a warm spot until double in bulk. Punch down dough; knead lightly a few times more to get the remaining gas out. Divide dough in half and form into long loaves. Place on a well-greased cookie sheet, and let rise again until double in bulk. Slash the top gently with a very sharp knife. Place in preheated oven for 30–35 minutes until loaves are brown and sound hollow when "thunked" with your fingers.

Cinnamon-Sourdough Bread

BAKING TIME: *30–35 minutes*
OVEN TEMPERATURE: *375 degrees*

Sponge:
> 1½ cups warm water
> 1 teaspoon granulated sugar
> 1 cup sourdough starter
> 2 cups bread flour

Bread:
> ½ cup granulated sugar
> 1 teaspoon salt
> 3 cups bread flour

Filling:
> 3 tablespoons butter, melted
> 2 teaspoons cinnamon
> 3 tablespoons granulated sugar
> ¼ cup raisins (optional)

Mix sponge ingredients. Stir well, place in a nonmetal bowl, and cover with plastic wrap. Set aside until mix is bubbly, about 8–12 hours.

To make bread, add sugar, salt and flour to fermenting sponge. Knead the dough for about 10 minutes until elastic, or until the dough bounces back when poked. Let rise in a warm spot until double in bulk. Punch down dough; knead lightly a few times more to get the remaining gas out. Divide dough in half and roll out to about ½ inch in thickness.

Brush one side with butter. Blend

(continued on following page)

THE FAVORED FLAVOR

By the mid-1800s, shipping and trading in the Old West had improved to the point of bringing many spices to the general population at affordable prices. A few spices became such standards that

manufacturers created spice boxes with prelabeled tin canisters.

Manufacturers did not forget chuck wagon cooks or traveling pioneers. They developed special spice boxes that would withstand the rough journey. Ingredients were essentially double-boxed to prevent loss by spillage and to provide protection against the elements.

In both cases, cinnamon was always one of the prelabeled containers included in the set. It was one spice travelers would not leave behind.

cinnamon and sugar, then sprinkle evenly over buttered dough. Add ¼ cup raisins per loaf, if desired. Roll up like a jelly roll, place in a well-greased loaf pan, and let rise again until double in bulk. Place in preheated oven for 30–35 minutes until loaves are brown and sound hollow when "thunked" with your fingers.

THE SOURDOUGH BARREL

Regardless of the kind of biscuit or bread flour used by cattle drive cooks, the starter came from the priceless chuck wagon sourdough barrel, and no "cookie" worth his title would be without one.

At the beginning of each drive, a watertight five-gallon barrel was set aside. The cook spent hours scrubbing and cleaning it to ensure no contamination. Then, using the spotless barrel as a mixing bowl, he added three to four quarts of flour, a dash of salt, and enough warm water to make a mash. After blending it well, he covered the keg and placed it in a warm spot to "start." The sun worked wonders. The starter mix captured airborne bacteria, which began batter fermentation. Often, "Cookie" threw away the first mix, believing the barrel needed a sour seasoning.

As the barrel contents were depleted, hardened batter streaked and splashed down its sides from the rough wagon ride. Although the barrel's appearance was lacking in aesthetics, bouncing around actually helped the contents mix thoroughly. It also clearly identified one of the most important containers on the chuck wagon.

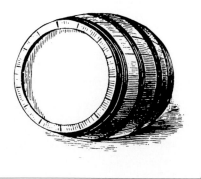

Whole Wheat Sourdough

BAKING TIME: *30–35 minutes*
OVEN TEMPERATURE: *375 degrees*

Sponge:
    1 ½ cups warm water
    1 teaspoon granulated sugar
    1 cup sourdough starter
    2 cups whole wheat flour
Bread:
    2 teaspoons salt
    3 cups whole wheat flour

Mix sponge ingredients. Stir well, place in a nonmetal bowl, and cover with plastic wrap. Set aside until mix is bubbly, about 8–12 hours.

To make bread, add salt and flour to fermenting sponge. Knead the dough for about 10 minutes until elastic, or until it bounces back when poked with your finger. Let rise in a warm spot until double in bulk. Punch down dough; knead lightly a few times more to get the remaining gas out. Divide dough in half and form into round loaves. Place on a well-greased cookie sheet, and let rise again until double in bulk. Slash the top gently with a very sharp knife. Place in preheated oven for 30–35 minutes until loaves are brown and sound hollow when "thunked" with your fingers.

THE CHUCK WAGON

Food wagons were in use since 1840 or so. However, it didn't take long for a creative entrepreneur to develop the first dedicated chuck wagon. Charles Goodnight made a sturdy version in 1866 with all the bells and whistles a cook could want. There were special compartments for storage and cleaning, a re-inforced drive train to ensure the cook would make it to the next stop, and a fold down table on the rear for food preparation.

For larger drives, a number of chuck wagons would accompany the trip with each feeding about eight to ten riders. The cook pre-pared each meal at the head of the drive, so he would have to position himself among the cattle at least twice a day. Because he rarely had time to rig any shelter, it must have given new meaning to camping.

Hornos Bread

Pueblo Indians and other tribes of the American plains developed a highly efficient and compact oven to rival any of the period. Called beehive ovens, or hornos, *they were compact, dome-shaped structures made of adobe. The hard-packed, sun-baked clay acted as an insulator for the tremendous heat generated by brush used to build the fire.*

After the horno was brought to temperature, the embers were brushed out the bread put in to bake. The oven's opening was covered with a sheepskin flap to hold radiant heat. A talented hand knew just when the bread was done.

You can do even better with this classic bread in a modern oven. Developed by Southwestern plains tribes after their introduction to wheat flour, there are numerous variations of this basic wheat bread. This is one of the easiest.

When correctly assembled, it will be a very dense bread. If you desire a lighter version, mix half white flour with half the designated whole wheat flour. For a crispy hornos crust, spray bread top with water about every 10 minutes while baking.

BAKING TIME: *30 minutes*
OVEN TEMPERATURE: *350 degrees*

Sponge:
  1½ cups warm water
  1 cup sourdough starter
  1 cup whole wheat flour
Bread:
  1 teaspoon salt
  3–4 cups whole wheat flour

Mix sponge ingredients. Stir well, place in a nonmetal bowl, and cover with plastic wrap. Set aside until mix is bubbly, about 8–12 hours.

To make bread, add the salt and flour to the fermenting sponge. Knead the dough for about 10 minutes until elastic, or until the dough bounces back when poked. Let rise in a warm spot until double in bulk. Punch down dough; knead lightly a few times more to get the remaining gas out. Divide dough in half and form into round loaves. Place on a well-greased cookie sheet, and let rise again until double in bulk. Slash the top gently with a very sharp knife. Place in preheated oven for 30 minutes until loaves are brown and sound hollow when "thunked" with your fingers.

Mock Sourdough

BAKING TIME: *30 minutes*
OVEN TEMPERATURE: *350 degrees*

Mock starter:
>   2 cups all-purpose flour
>   3 tablespoons granulated sugar
>   1 teaspoon salt
>   2 cups water
>   1 package dry yeast
>   1 tablespoon vinegar

Bread:
>   3 cups all-purpose flour
>   1 teaspoon baking soda

Mix all ingredients of the mock starter, and stir with a whisk until well blended. Put aside for a few hours; it should sour quickly. When it has reached the proper "aroma" (soured to your satisfaction), mix in bread ingredients (flour and baking soda). Knead well and let rise until double in bulk. Divide, place into two 9-inch loaf pans, and let rise again. When the dough fills the bread pan, place in preheated oven for 35 minutes until loaves are golden brown and sound hollow when "thunked" with your fingers.

VARIATION
↝ Use whole wheat flour as a substitute for all-purpose and add one tablespoon brown sugar.

Sourdough was astoundingly popular with Old West residents. When tragedy struck and the starter was lost, the dilemma was what to do while another was being made. An ingenious baker, obviously faced with this calamity, developed a substitute. His (or her) souring ingredient was vinegar. Just a dash did all the work. The pungent odor didn't exactly hold the same sweet sourdough undertones, but sometimes there wasn't enough time to impress cowpokes with the real stuff.

Here's a compilation of an old recipe or two that made a quick sourdough when the ranch hands were screaming for more. It will make rolls as well as loaves of bread. This modern recipe is also given a boost with dry yeast.

Oatmeal-Apple Sourdough

erved by virtually all Old West bakers, sourdough baked goods were a delicious departure from the mundane. Better yet, their popularity allowed for some extremely creative endeavors.

Oats and apples were in abundance in fall months, so what better marriage than in a loaf of sourdough. The outline for this appeared in a recipe book written in 1885. It's a bit different from a typical loaf. Incorporating cooking spices normally found on every chuck wagon traveling the range, it's as close to an apple pie as bread can get.

It keeps superbly and is tasty as a sandwich bread or just by itself.

BAKING TIME: 30–35 minutes
OVEN TEMPERATURE: 375 degrees

Sponge:
 ½ cup warm water
 1 teaspoon sugar
 1 cup sourdough starter
 2 cups all-purpose or bread flour
Bread:
 2 cups shredded apple
 ½ cup granulated sugar
 ¼ teaspoon nutmeg
 1 teaspoon cinnamon
 ¼ teaspoon cloves
 1 teaspoon salt
 1 teaspoon vanilla
 ½ cup milk
 1 cup rolled oats
 2–3 cups all-purpose flour

Mix sponge ingredients. Stir well and place in a nonmetal bowl and cover with plastic wrap. Set aside until mix is bubbly, about 8–12 hours.

To make bread, peel, core, and grate apples. Place in a bowl and add apples, sugar, nutmeg, cinnamon, cloves, salt, and vanilla. Let sit for about 5 minutes. Add milk, oats, and flour to the sponge, and mix thoroughly. Now work in apple mixture and knead dough lightly for about 5 minutes until slightly elastic. Let rise in a warm spot until double in bulk. Punch down dough; knead lightly a few times more to get the remaining gas out. Divide dough in half. Place into two well-greased loaf pans and let rise again until double in bulk. Place in preheated oven for 30–35 minutes until loaves are brown and sound hollow when "thunked" with your fingers.

Sweet Potato Bread

BAKING TIME: *30–35 minutes*
OVEN TEMPERATURE: *375 degrees*

Sponge:
  2 cups warm milk
  1 tablespoon granulated sugar
  1 cup sourdough starter
  2 cups all-purpose flour
Bread:
  2 medium sweet potatoes
  1 teaspoon salt
  3 cups all-purpose flour

Mix sponge ingredients. Stir well, place in a nonmetal bowl, and cover with plastic wrap. Set aside until mix is bubbly, about 8–12 hours.

To make bread, peel and boil sweet potatoes in lightly salted water. They are done when a fork slips easily into the potato, about 15 minutes. Mash through a colander as they did in the Old West, or

(continued on following page)

Sweet potatoes were very easy to grow in most areas, and what couldn't be grown could be acquired through inexpensive shopping or bartering. Sweet potatoes kept well and could accept any number of spices, so few tired of the taste. They were truly one of the most versatile foods in the West.

Rather than serve the potato simply as a table vegetable, most people used it in a variety of dishes. Especially popular were sweet potato desserts such as pies, cakes, and puddings. In breads, they added not only essential nutrients, but color and taste as well. Sweet Potato Bread was almost a meal unto itself.

In this recipe, the bread is so rich it's almost an after-dinner treat. It easily could serve as a center for lunch on the trail. It is moist and keeps well.

puree in a food processor. Add puree, salt, and flour to the fermenting sponge. Knead the dough for about 10 minutes until elastic, or until it bounces back when poked with your finger. It may require more flour because of the potatoes. Let rise in a warm spot until double in bulk. Punch down dough; knead lightly a few times more to get the remaining gas out. Divide dough in half and form into round loaves. Place on a well-greased cookie sheet, and let rise again until double in bulk. Slash the tops with a sharp knife. Place in preheated oven for 30–35 minutes until loaves are brown and sound hollow when "thunked" with your fingers.

EATIN' IRONS IN THE WRECK PAN

One would think open range dust, dirt, and mud would cause enough frustration that conditions around the chuck wagon and ranch homes would rival the desert itself. Not so. Most Old West cooks went to extraordinary efforts to keep food areas free from "smell" and obvious dirt.

Aprons worn by cooks were usually old flour or sugar sacks. The all-purpose flour sacks also filled in as dish towels. They were regularly cleaned and rinsed in the local creek or in well-water pans.

Leftover food was not to be brought anywhere near the chuck wagon because of the insects it would draw. If by some rare chance a cowboy or range worker did not finish his meal, he was expected to scrape his scraps into the fire or leave them for the wildlife. Birds often followed the chuck wagon with such expectations.

Scraped eatin' irons and tin plates were deposited into a large pan known as the "wreck pan" or "roundup pan" for the cook to clean up later. Pots and pans were scrubbed out daily with hot water and lye soap. If they were really a mess, lye soap and sand would knock out the chunks. The food area was constantly brushed down and scraped clean with a sharp knife.

Potato Bread

BAKING TIME: *35–45 minutes*
OVEN TEMPERATURE: *375 degrees*

Sponge:
  ½ cup warm water
  1 tablespoon granulated sugar
  2 cups potato sourdough starter
  2 cups bread flour
Bread:
  1 cup mashed or instant potatoes
  2 tablespoons butter, melted
  2 teaspoons salt
  2 cups bread flour

Mix sponge ingredients. Stir well, place in a nonmetal bowl and cover with plastic wrap. Set aside until mix is bubbly, about 8–12 hours.

To make bread, add cooled mashed potatoes, butter, salt, and flour to the fermenting sponge. Add water if necessary. Knead dough for about 10 minutes until elastic, or until the dough bounces back when poked. Let rise in a warm spot until double in bulk. Punch down dough; knead lightly a few times more to get the remaining gas out. Divide dough in half and form into loaves. Place on a well-greased loaf pan and let rise again until double in bulk. Slash the top with a sharp knife. Place in preheated oven for 35–45 minutes until loaves are brown and sound hollow when "thunked" with your fingers.

Potatoes are thought to have originated in Peru, carried to Europe in the sixteenth century, then introduced into the American colonies with settlers in the early 1600s. The plant proved so hardy and prolific, potatoes became a staple in American life—so it was only natural that they joined pioneers traveling to the West.

As pioneers quickly discovered, one of the advantages of potatoes was their ability to condition bread dough to cover faults found in low-quality or low-grade flours. This was a significant issue during pioneer transits. But potatoes had other advantages. They were versatile, kept well, had significant amounts of vitamin C, and were relatively inexpensive.

Due to weight, most potatoes were picked up at local markets en route to the West. Chuck wagon cooks had no such shopping privileges, so potato dishes were generally served early in the cattle drive.

This recipe is a basic sourdough bread. To heighten flavor, it is made with potato starter.

Sour Cream Biscuits

BAKING TIME: *15 minutes*
OVEN TEMPERATURE: *400 degrees*

1 cup sourdough starter
½ cup water
1 cup sour cream
1 egg, beaten
3–4 cups all-purpose flour
1 teaspoon salt
1 teaspoon granulated sugar
2 teaspoons baking soda

It may sound like a whole bunch of "soured" ingredients, but the recipe is really quite harmless.

In the Old West, soured milk and cream were used with baking soda to allow the soda to do its work. Soured dairy goods also produced lactic acid, which resulted in a very tender bread or biscuit crumb. These biscuits also used up any soured milk not fit for drinking. Although their popularity was undeniable, they are difficult to duplicate in today's recipes. In the past, soured cream was easy and safe to use. Today, if one were to try souring with pasteurized cream, it would generally spoil and skip the souring stage. To duplicate the taste as close as possible, processed sour cream is a safe alternative. Another method is to add a teaspoon of vinegar to one cup of whole milk. It will taste much like sour milk.

These biscuits are rich and finely textured. Adding baking soda gives the biscuit a quick boost.

Blend sourdough starter, water, sour cream, and egg in a large bowl. In a separate bowl, blend remaining ingredients. Add the dry ingredients in thirds to the starter mix, stirring lightly between each addition. Add more water if necessary. Turn out on floured board and knead briefly until just mixed. Rub hands in flour and pat out dough on lightly floured flat surface to about ½ inch thick. Cut with a biscuit cutter or upside-down glass. Be sure to dip the cutter in flour before each use so the biscuit dough won't stick. Place on a greased cookie sheet and let rise an hour. Place in preheated oven and bake until lightly brown. Serve immediately.

Sourdough Gems

BAKING TIME: *20 minutes*

OVEN TEMPERATURE: *400 degrees*

> *1 cup sourdough starter*
> *½ cup buttermilk*
> *3 cups whole wheat flour*
> *1 teaspoon salt*
> *1 tablespoon granulated sugar*
> *2 teaspoons baking soda*

Blend sourdough starter and buttermilk in a large bowl. In a separate bowl, blend flour, salt, sugar, and baking soda. Add the dry ingredients in thirds to the starter mix, stirring lightly between each addition. Turn out onto lightly floured board and knead briefly until just mixed. Scoop out an ice-cream-dipper-sized piece of batter, and place in well-greased muffin pan. Be sure to dunk the dipper in flour before each use so the biscuit won't stick. Let rise an hour or so, and place in a preheated oven. Bake until lightly brown and gems spring back to the touch. Serve immediately.

*M*ost muffinlike gems were made with baking soda or baking powder. The sourdough added to this recipe wasn't necessarily for leavening, but flavor. It added a nice tang to the usual gem.

The original recipe writer was very proud of her creation. At the end of her assembly instructions she stated, "To a natural, healthy appetite no item of the gourmand's feast can be more tempting nor eaten with keener relish." The term gourmand *is not necessarily flattering by modern standards, since it is defined as one loving to feast, but because of the day's hard work, many homesteaders and pioneers were prone to excessive eating. This is understandable since the next meal was never guaranteed. Unlike bread, a smaller gem could be carried easily in a pouch for later consumption in the fields or ahead of the covered wagon.*

Gems were baked in special pans, but for this assembly, use a muffin pan. This is similar to an original gem pan, and works well.

THAT DANG NEW OVEN

Until a baker became used to the new cooking gadget erected in the ranch house kitchen, creative efforts often went astray. First attempts at bread in the new oven were usually the most entertaining. Initial results were often described in personal logs as well-done bricks, and one hapless baker couldn't cut his product with a knife, so he took it outside to use "a hatchet to make any impression." That didn't work either, so he baked three new loaves before he got even close to making palatable bread. The ranch hands didn't say a word.

Sourdough-Molasses Bread

BAKING TIME: *35 minutes*
OVEN TEMPERATURE: *375 degrees*

Sponge:
　　2 cups warm water
　　½ cup powdered milk
　　1 cup sourdough starter
　　1 cup whole wheat flour
Bread:
　　1 teaspoon salt
　　¼ cup molasses
　　3–4 cups whole wheat flour

Mix sponge ingredients, ensuring powdered milk is completely dissolved. Stir well, place in a nonmetal bowl and cover with plastic wrap. Set aside until mix is bubbly, about 8–12 hours.

To make the bread, mix salt, molasses, and flour with the sponge. Add more water if necessary. Knead until elastic; it will take longer than a normal loaf because of the whole wheat flour. If the dough is too sticky to knead, coat hands with vegetable oil and continue kneading. Let rise in warm place until double in bulk, at least an hour or more. Punch down and place onto well-greased cookie sheets. Bake in preheated oven until done to a golden brown and sounds hollow when "thunked" with your fingers.

Sylvester Graham Bread

BAKING TIME: *30–35 minutes*
OVEN TEMPERATURE: *375 degrees*

Sponge:
> 2 cups warm water
> ¼ cup molasses
> 1 cup sourdough starter
> 2 cups graham flour

Bread:
> 1 teaspoon salt
> 3 cups graham flour

Mix sponge ingredients. Stir well, place in a nonmetal bowl, and cover with plastic wrap. Set aside until mix is bubbly, about 8–12 hours.

To make bread, add salt and flour to fermenting sponge. Knead the dough for about 10 minutes until elastic, or until the dough bounces back when poked. Let rise in a warm spot until double in bulk. Punch down dough; knead lightly a few times more to get the remaining gas out. Divide dough in half and form into round loaves. Place on a well-greased cookie sheet, and let rise again until double in bulk. Slash the top gently with a very sharp knife. Place in preheated oven for 30–35 minutes until loaves are brown and sound hollow when "thunked" with your fingers.

By sifting or "bolting" flour, what was believed to be the prime portion of the wheat berry could be sold at premium prices. Of course, only the elite could afford such an extravagance as white flour. The remaining flour portions went to the middle class and the poor.

In the mid-1800s, Sylvester Graham advocated the use of the whole grain in baked goods—bran and all. His reasoning was that the entire berry contained nutrients, so why sift it out. As wagons traveled west and picked up supplies at major outposts, "graham flour" was generally available, but only those seeking healthy foods would search it out; fashion still dictated "pure" white flour, if one had the money.

Since graham flour required less milling, it was considerably cheaper to manufacture. Clever marketing people sold it under other names, so most traveling west used it whether they realized it or not.

Although the result is now labeled "whole wheat," graham flour is still available in health food stores. The special milling of graham flour is more true to the Old West than the milling of whole wheat, producing a denser loaf.

Sourdough Yeast Biscuits

Probably no other food in the Old West was more written about, talked about, and loved than sourdough biscuits. Not a personal journal or other writing ends without a reference made to morning sourdough biscuits. A chuck wagon cook's reputation was centered on how he baked biscuits. For a cook who couldn't conjure up a great batch of steaming sourdough, it was a long trip of constant harassment from his customers.

There are as many recipes for sourdough biscuits as cooks, but the kinds of ingredients are relatively consistent. This recipe is a compilation of many good blends. They are soft and chewy, so just imagine yourself sitting by a campfire watching over three thousand head of cattle.

BAKING TIME: *15 minutes*
OVEN TEMPERATURE: *400 degrees*

Sponge:
  1 cup buttermilk
  1 tablespoon granulated sugar
  1 cup sourdough starter
  2 cups all-purpose flour
Bread:
  2 tablespoons butter or margarine
  1 tablespoon granulated sugar
  1 tablespoon baking powder
  1 teaspoon salt
  1 cup all-purpose flour

Mix sponge ingredients. Stir well, place in a nonmetal bowl, and cover with plastic wrap. Set aside until mix is bubbly, about 8–12 hours.

To make biscuits, melt butter and stir in sugar until well blended. Add all remaining ingredients to the sponge and knead the dough for about 10 minutes until elastic or until it bounces back when poked. Let rise in a warm spot until double in bulk. Punch down dough; knead lightly a few times more to get the remaining gas out. Pat out to ½ inch thick and cut out biscuits with a biscuit cutter. Place on a well-greased cookie sheet and let rise again until double in bulk. Place in preheated oven for 15 minutes or until the tops are golden brown.

English Yeast Muffins

BAKING TIME: *10 minutes*
OVEN TEMPERATURE: *400 degrees*

1 cup sourdough starter
1 cup buttermilk
1 egg, beaten
3 cups all-purpose flour
1 tablespoon granulated sugar
1 teaspoon baking soda
1 teaspoon salt
1 tablespoon vegetable oil or butter

In a large bowl, blend starter, buttermilk, and egg. In another bowl, stir together flour, sugar, baking soda, and salt. Pour dry ingredients into the starter; mix in thirds, blending as you pour. Do not over-mix. Prepare a large skillet with vegetable oil or butter, and place well-greased muffin rings in the skillet. Form a golf ball–sized piece of dough, and sprinkle with cornmeal. Place directly into the rings and flatten if necessary. Bake until light brown and turn over, about 5 minutes per side. When done, place on a wire rack to cool.

The English muffins purchased today bear little resemblance to those made by nineteenth-century bakers. In the Old West, English muffins were baked in rings placed on a hot skillet. They baked quickly and formed numerous air bubbles, many of which are visible on the top of the muffin.

Due to the rapid baking, the sourdough starter is used for flavoring more than leavening. The muffin gets a boost from baking powder, which doesn't change the taste, but yields a lighter product. English Yeast Muffins break apart nicely with a fork. Slicing them with a knife was considered a travesty because fork-splitting revealed more nooks and crannies to hold butter or jam.

American bakers always used cornmeal on the top and bottom of the muffin. It's now almost a necessity for authenticity, so plan on sprinkling the skillet with cornmeal before pouring batter. Use muffin rings to hold the dough. If none are to be found, use an old tuna-fish can cut out on top and bottom.

Salt-Rising Bread: An Old West Standby

AS PROLIFIC AS SOURDOUGH WAS IN THE OLD WEST, THERE would always come a time when no starter was available. At that point, baking soda would be substituted as a leavening agent. Although baking soda breads were crumbly, they were certainly adequate for those with a robust appetite.

With few, if any, food stores within a reasonable walking distance, sometimes even baking soda was nowhere to be found. In that case, pioneers dusted off an old standby recipe. Called salt-rising bread, it was a popular and simple alternative. The leavening agent was the flour itself, and it often resolved the quandary of how to assemble a palatable loaf of bread when no leavening agents were available. On the down side, results were extremely unpredictable. Leavening action was highly dependent on flour quality, temperature, and assembly.

Although flours milled during the nineteenth century were reasonably easy to obtain, they varied wildly in purity. If the consumer were lucky and the flour high in gluten (protein), the results could be spectacular. Breads made from this flour were easy to handle and assemble, light in texture, and delicious. However, flour containing dirt and rocks, certainly less than ideal baking properties, was more likely. For some, it was more like assembling a loaf with building material instead of flour, but they made do.

What Is "Salt-Rising"?

Salt-rising doesn't mean extra salt in the dough or a heavy salty taste. There are at least two stories on the origin of the name.

Pictured, clockwise from upper left, are Sourdough-Molasses Bread (page 60), Salt-Rising Bread (page 68), Sylvester Graham rolls (page 61), and Mock Sourdough rolls (page 53).

One story is that salt was believed to enhance fermentation, so it was added to the sponge early in assembly. In reality, it arrests fermentation, but it is necessary to help control rapid rising that would make for weak dough. Right ingredient, wrong reason. Another story states that salt-rising refers to the original method of getting the dough to a constant temperature. A pan of fresh dough would sit in a warm bed of salt to ferment. The even, long-lasting heat retention of salt would impart the most desirable environment for the dough to mature.

Thus, salt-rising bread is a very close cousin to sourdough because the starter is fermented by airborne microbes, the same as sourdough. However, the American version of salt-rising generally uses cornmeal as a base and is a one-shot process. Unlike sourdough, all the sponge is used up in one recipe.

How Is It Made?

Nineteenth-century bakers used a number of different processes. But with so little control over the quality of available flour, it was no small task baking two loaves the same height. Although the technique should have been impractical for wagon train or chuck wagon cooks because of the need for temperature control, they often made it with wonderful results.

By assembling the starter before the morning departure and packing the pans of wet flour in an insulation of clothes or blankets, the cooks ensured that the blend would ferment wonderfully. The bouncing and rolling of the wagons during the fermentation continually mixed the sponge, resulting in very active mix. The outcome was baked in a Dutch oven that evening for fresh dinner bread.

This process was far easier in an old ranch house. There, stoves were mostly stoked throughout the day since it was so hard to warm up the heavy cast metal. Placed near the stove with ideal even heat, warm dough could be ignored and still develop nicely. The pungent odor of active fermentation was a welcome signal that bread was almost ready for the oven.

Making Your Own

Putting salt-rising bread together is not a formidable task, but it is so wildly unpredictable that it does depend a bit on luck. To increase the odds of success, try the following:

- Do not boost the growth of starter with any yeast. It may rise, but it will destroy the unique flavoring.
- Keep the starter warming, about 90–100 degrees if possible. Try putting it next to your hot water heater or on a warming tray.
- Start on a small scale. Don't make so much that it can't work to get itself going. Better to try a little and use the result in a larger batch.
- Remember, this is a slow process, but if you get no action after twenty-four hours, toss it and start again.

The best of luck in your exploration of a wonderful old leavening process. May all your loaves be tall.

Hopi woman grinding corn, ca. 1910.

Salt-Rising Bread

reshly stone-ground cornmeal works best. However, it is not always an easy item to find today, so use the finest available. If fermentation goes nowhere, refer to sourdough starters (pages 46–47) in this chapter and add ½ cup to the cornmeal mix. This is cheating a bit, but will give it a kick start and the same delicious flavor and fine texture.

BAKING TIME: *35 minutes*
OVEN TEMPERATURE: *375 degrees*

Salt-rising starter:
    ½ cup cornmeal
    1 teaspoon granulated sugar
    1 cup buttermilk
Salt-rising bread:
    1½ cups buttermilk
    3 tablespoons granulated sugar
    2 teaspoons salt
    5–7 cups bread flour

To make the starter, stir cornmeal and sugar to blend. Warm milk and mix with cornmeal blend. Set in warm spot for 24 hours to allow fermentation. The starter should have expanded and have a nice aroma. If the mix is not light and bubbly, give it another 24 hours, or add ½ cup sourdough starter and set aside in a warm spot for an additional 12 hours. It must be kept warm.

To make the bread, pour complete starter, buttermilk, sugar, salt, and 3 cups of flour into a large bowl. Mix thoroughly, cover with plastic wrap, and let ferment an additional 3–4 hours, sometimes longer if the area is cool. When light and bubbly, add remaining flour to make a moderately stiff dough. Knead until elastic, about 10 minutes. Grease bowl and place the dough

(continued on following page)

back in for a third rising. When about double in bulk, or a finger hole stays in the dough after it's been pressed, divide into two equal pieces. Roll out the remaining air. Place the dough into two well-greased 9-inch loaf pans, or make into two round loaves and place on a cookie sheet. Let rise once again. Place in preheated oven when double in bulk. When loaves are lightly browned and sound hollow when "thunked" with your fingers, remove from pan and cool on wire rack.

CORN BEER

Corn beer proceeded the distillates early settlers brought to the Old West. The Western Apache and Chiricahua created "Tula-pah," and prepared it much like European hops-based beer. Corn sprouts were dug up, dried, and pulverized. Local flavoring was mixed in, usually locoweed or rootbark of some specialized plant.

The entire mixture was boiled in water until a foam was formed. The foam was poured off into a separate pot, and the remaining mash pulverized once again. It was combined once more for boiling, and allowed to cool and ferment for twelve to twenty-four hours. The mix spoiled quickly, so it was consumed in short order.

Aside from the obvious pleasurable side effects of the ethanol created in the mix, it was declared a nutritional and medicinal wonder. On the down side, it was also a very powerful laxative.

ALL IN A DAY'S WORK

A typical wagon train day started just before dawn. Men gathered herds of oxen and companion cattle, tying them close by. Then they carefully checked over the "prairie schooners" for the day's journey while women readied the campfire, boiled kettles of water with coffee grounds, and warmed beans. Bread made from the night before, or fresh suckeyes (pancakes), augmented strong coffee. Some milk from accompanying cows was available during the first part of the trip, but later in the journey, the cows were slaughtered for meat.

By the time dawn broke, the prairie schooners were loaded and the oxen hitched. The wagons began their movement. There was little to do crawling along at a few miles per hour, but the men generally guided the oxen train while enterprising women completed mending and preparation for the next meal. It was even possible to prepare biscuits and roll out pie dough on the large bench seat. The slow speed allowed gathering of cow chips, wood, and weeds for a fire that evening. If the gatherer was very lucky, he might spot berries for a tart or pie.

Lunch was a cold meal of leftovers from dinner or bread baked the evening before. Little time was wasted when another two miles' travel was possible.

On a fair day, dinner was the regal meal of the day. The campfire was started with copious amounts of cow or buffalo chips. Two fork sticks were driven into the ground on each side of the fire with a pole laid across them for suspending kettles or pots. The evening's bill of fare might include biscuits, salted pork, or game caught along the way. On the side were beans or rice and stewed fruit or some creative dish for dessert. Early in the journey, potatoes and other vegetables were available. Unfortunately, by the end of the trip supplies on hand rarely went beyond beans, hot crackers, and bacon.

Finally, they had to get ready for the next day's journey: mend clothes, do laundry, and repack the wagon. This four to six months of camping made for some very sturdy western settlers.

Cakes
Making History

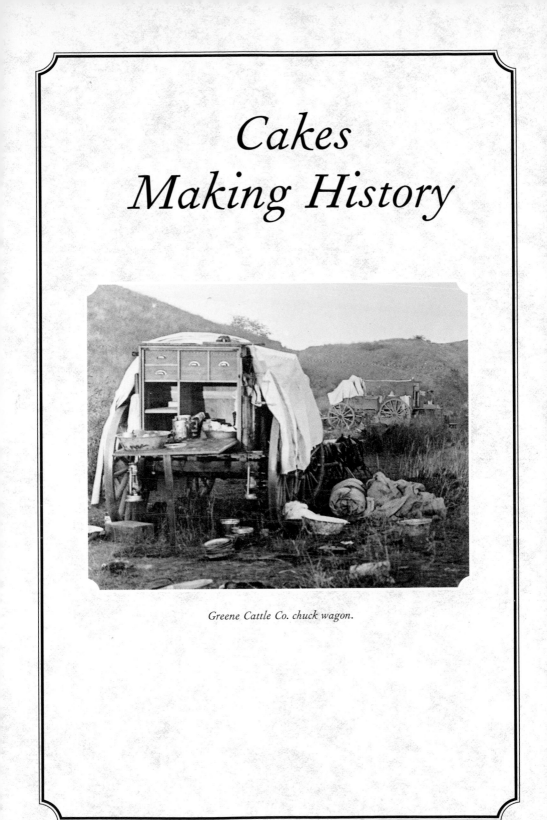

Greene Cattle Co. chuck wagon.

Cakes: A Wonder of the West

S O MUCH HAS BEEN WRITTEN AND DISCUSSED ABOUT CAKES, IT'S easy to lose sight of how difficult it was to create this marvelous treat on the open range. Procedures for blending and baking cakes were well established by the time Old West residents set up camp. The problem was to modify ingredients and control temperature to make do with the primitive equipment.

Whereas bakers in large East Coast cities served as fine a variety of complicated cakes as we see today, Western bakers were a bit more basic. Any inclination homesteaders had to assemble exquisitely decorated cakes was certainly left at their home back east. There was neither the equipment, nor the ingredients, nor the time to prepare picture-perfect results, so cakes were made not only with indigenous material, but also baked in the worst possible conditions.

Journals of the era indicate ranch house bakers and some open range cooks did a credible job at making tender and flavorful cakes. They just looked a bit different. A fine example of just how far one could go with mixes was the One-Egg Cake. Eggs, so necessary to cake texture, were at a premium. The one-egg cake made maximum use of a precious commodity and produced a very palatable product. Chuck wagon cooks also found that a new leavening agent called "yeast powder" helped make a decent cake in a Dutch oven immersed in embers. Before the introduction of this baking powder, yeast-based cakes were popular and somewhat distinctive in flavor. The sourdough yeast imparted an interesting aroma usually attributed to biscuits.

With so many variables found in making cakes, rarely did a recipe book include directions for assembly. Ingredients were listed, but it was thought the baker should already know how to blend them. Also, because every oven was

Pictured, clockwise from upper left, are Railroad Cake (page 85), Classic Pound Cake (page 78), and Spice Cake (page 86).

totally dependent on the baker's adept hand, it was impossible to recommend a temperature other than "bake in a medium-warm stove."

Preparation

Blending and baking cakes in contemporary kitchens hold many of the same rules bakers of the Old West ascribed to:

- ∽ Always use the highest quality materials available.
- ∽ Pay attention to the measurements and ensure all ingredients make it into the cake.
- ∽ Use the oven temperature recommended in the recipe. Slower baking will dry the cake, and faster baking (higher temperature) will produce a finely granulated raw one.
- ∽ All ingredients should be at room temperature prior to mixing.

Mixing

Nothing ruins a cake faster than under- or overmixing. Blending isn't an exact science, so it's difficult to make hard rules. The good news is that the window of opportunity to do it properly is broad enough that everyone should get the it right. As a guideline, with all ingredients at room temperature, mixing should not take less than one minute or longer than three minutes. This includes adding and blending. Ideal mixing tools are a slotted wooden spoon and a wire whisk. These are basically the same tools used in the Old West, so they must be good.

When Is It Done?

The following came from directions in one of the larger nineteenth-century western cookbooks: "[to tell] when cake is done, take a fine clean broom splint and pass it into the center of the cake to see if it comes out dry."

Not much has changed. Today a toothpick or knife accomplishes the same thing and is still one of the most reliable methods. Other indications include nicely browned edges pulling away from the side of the pan and cake spring back when pushed down lightly. Keep a close eye on the time. If it appears done too early or too late, check the oven temperature. Finally, if the cake was not assembled with ingredients at room temperature, it will take longer to bake.

Apple Cake

BAKING TIME: *45 minutes*

OVEN TEMPERATURE: *350 degrees*

1 cup brown sugar
½ cup butter or margarine
2 cups all-purpose flour
2 teaspoons baking powder
½ teaspoon salt
1 teaspoon cinnamon
1 teaspoon ground cloves
2 eggs, beaten
1 cup applesauce
1 cup raisins

Cream sugar and butter until light and fluffy. In a separate bowl, mix flour, baking powder, salt, cinnamon, and cloves. Add dry ingredients to the butter mix in thirds, alternating with eggs and applesauce. Mix thoroughly. Stir in raisins. Bake in one of two ways. To make a stacking cake, grease and flour two 8-inch cake pans and split batter. For applesauce loaves, pour batter into two well-greased and floured bread loaf pans. Place in preheated oven. Done when toothpick inserted into cake comes out dry.

As a round cake, best served with a cream cheese icing. Out of loaf pans, sprinkle with powdered sugar when cool.

(continued on following page)

This country has embraced apples as a delight second to none. We grow more apples than any other nation, and hundreds of recipes are printed every fall offering creative uses for the popular fruit. The history of the Old West is laced with apples. It wasn't just apple pie that was so popular. Apples appeared in hundreds of Old West dishes. They could be added to vegetable dishes, puddings, and just about anything else cooking over a campfire.

For use in a cake, apples were plentiful and easy to prepare. They helped provide a valuable sweetener and additional moisture to the cake. Applesauce was the simplest way to add apples to a cake. Anyone with a fire could cook down apples for a mush to mush. Today, the easiest way to process applesauce is to puree cooked apples in a food processor. For this recipe, fresh apples are decidedly tastier. Check Variations after the recipe for cooking apples. However, if short of time, use a high-quality, natural applesauce available at most health food stores.

VARIATIONS

∽ Add half a cup of chopped walnuts or pecans with applesauce.

∽ To make your own applesauce, peel and core apples. Then place apples in a roasting pan and immerse them in ½ inch of hot water. Add 2 tablespoons sugar and place in a 450 degree oven for 30 minutes. Puree until smooth.

"FREIGHTING" THE GOODS

What we take for granted—fresh vegetables, fruits and staples—was not so eas-ily obtained one hundred years ago. Prior to the building of the railroad, supplies reached Old West outposts by wagon. "Freighting" came in from suppliers by mule teams, so the freshness of any goods was certainly suspect.

California was the major exporter. They grew crops in abundance, and whatever couldn't be cultivated in the rich soil could be brought by ship to any one of numerous California ports. However, hauling goods from the coast into the outback wasn't a bargain. Teams of mules covered the Southwest on a regular basis for about ten cents a pound. This may not seem like much now, but when potatoes normally cost eight cents a pound, it more than doubled the price.

There were alternatives for settlers. Game was plentiful, and so were butter and milk because of all the range beef about. Crops indigenous to the area were grown, and spices helped perk up less than spectacular foods.

By 1870, the "Iron Horse" finally had its tracks laid, and the cost of goods dropped dramatically, putting most alternative freighting out of business.

Cheap Fruit Cake

BAKING TIME: *1 hour*
OVEN TEMPERATURE: *350 degrees*

1 cup granulated sugar
2 cups all-purpose flour
2 teaspoons baking powder
¼ teaspoon salt
¾ cup butter or margarine
1 teaspoon cinnamon
½ teaspoon mace
½ teaspoon ground cloves
¼ teaspoon nutmeg
1 cup water
1 cup raisins or currants

Stir sugar, flour, baking powder, and salt together. Cut in butter and mix until mealy. Then add spices and mix together. Add water ½ cup at a time and mix thoroughly, about 1½ minutes. Fold in raisins. Pour batter into a well-greased and floured 7-inch loaf pan, and bake in a preheated oven. Done when inserted toothpick comes out dry.

Slice thin like fruit cake.

VARIATIONS
⌐ If you're wealthy, add ½ cup chopped walnuts or pecans.
⌐ If you're very wealthy, substitute chopped dates for raisins.

There was an effort in many older recipes to duplicate favored dishes found back home. This, and the challenge for pioneers and new ranch cooks to use simple mixes in a demanding baking environment, made for unusual solutions. As a result, many recipes of the era were "make do." If a reasonably good-tasting product could come out of the ranch house oven, or could be made in a Dutch oven with available supplies, it was a recipe to be reckoned.

With cost and availability in mind, creators of this blend used lard for butter and water for milk, and they deleted the eggs. Very basic indeed. Titled *Cheap Fruit Cake* in a nineteenth-century midwestern cookbook, it was a solution to eating like "eastern folk," but *Cheap Fruit Cake* used the most inexpensive and most popular supplies available to western bakers.

Our recipe is a mix of a few popular selections except for the use of butter. However, feel free to use bear lard if it's in your pantry.

Classic Pound Cake

This recipe is truly one of the time-honored dishes, around for at least three hundred years. Immigrants brought it over on the first European boats to hit these shores and carried it west. The name evolved from the ingredients: one pound flour, one pound butter, one pound eggs, and one pound sugar. Certainly not a recipe easy to lose. Also called "butter cake," it was simple to prepare, had few ingredients, kept well, and would not fall apart or crush easily in transit. What more could a pioneer desire?

This recipe reflects the original intent of its creators. For those wanting to personalize the cake, see Variations.

BAKING TIME: *1 hour*
OVEN TEMPERATURE: *350 degrees*

2 cups granulated sugar
2 cups unsalted butter (4 sticks)
10 eggs
4½ cups all-purpose flour
1½ teaspoons salt
1 teaspoon baking powder
1 teaspoon vanilla

Cream sugar and butter. Add 2 eggs at a time and slowly blend. In a separate bowl, combine flour, salt, and baking powder. Blend well and add dry mix to egg mix, and beat well. Add vanilla to batter. Pour batter into two well-greased and floured 7-inch loaf pans or a 10-inch angel food cake pan to two-thirds full. Bake in a preheated oven. Done when inserted toothpick comes out dry; remove from oven and cool.

Hot or cold, this is delicious. Even better topped with fresh fruit, like strawberries. Freezes exceptionally well.

VARIATIONS
‿ For chocolate pound cake add ¼ cup cocoa to dry mix.
‿ Delete vanilla and add 1 tablespoon orange or lemon bits.

Coffee Cake

BAKING TIME: *35 minutes*
OVEN TEMPERATURE: *350 degrees*

1 cup granulated sugar
1 cup butter or margarine
2 cups whole wheat or all-purpose flour
2 teaspoons baking powder
¼ teaspoon nutmeg
¼ teaspoon cinnamon
½ teaspoon salt
½ cup molasses
½ cup cold coffee
½ cup cream
3 eggs, beaten
1 cup raisins

Cream sugar and butter until light and fluffy. In a separate bowl, mix flour, baking powder, spices, and salt. Add molasses, coffee, cream, and eggs; blend together. Slowly mix this into butter a bit at a time and blend. Stir in raisins and bake in a well-greased and floured 7-inch loaf pan. It's done when inserted toothpick comes out dry.

Slice and butter for a morning treat.

VARIATION
↪ Try a streusel topping: ¼ cup cold butter, ¼ cup brown sugar, ¼ teaspoon cinnamon. Cream butter and sugar until mealy, add cinnamon and flour. Mix well. Top coffee cake before placing in oven.

A PERFECT CUP

Preparing a cup of coffee didn't require much imagination, but it did take a deft hand to come out palatable.

It began with the ranch cook or chuck wagon gourmet roasting green coffee beans in a skillet. Sources suggest this was a task with highly suspect quality control since taste was directly dependent on roasting time and even temperature. Erratic fires were hard to control, so it took a skilled hand to know when to pull the beans out in time. Then, when the beans cooled, the cook ground them very course, about the consistency of oatmeal. It was believed the boiled coffee clarified itself from any remaining beans, as large grounds settled to the bottom.

Since a filled coffee pot typically spent hours boiling over a campfire, intensive quality control over roasting or grinding expensive coffee beans probably didn't make much difference in flavor.

Although ginger is the predominant spice in many Far Eastern dishes, it was also extremely popular in the Old West—so much so that special boxes were designed just to hold the spice. Gingerbread, ginger gems, and ginger pudding were all part of an Old West diet. It was also used as a spice for meats and vegetables, and made a delicious vinegar.

Fresh ginger was generally available to settled families in the big cities, but very difficult for the Old West cooks to find in quantity. Fortunately, manufacturing techniques of the time were advanced enough to allow for drying ginger and storing it in jars. Purity was sometimes questionable; but no matter, the convenience far outweighed any annoyance such as dirt.

This recipe is a step removed from classic gingerbread.

Ginger Cake

BAKING TIME: *35 minutes*
OVEN TEMPERATURE: *350 degrees*

1 cup granulated sugar
½ cup butter or margarine
2 eggs, beaten
1 cup sour cream
½ cup molasses
3 cups all-purpose flour
1 teaspoon baking soda
2 teaspoons ginger
1 teaspoon allspice

Cream sugar and butter. Mix in eggs. In a separate bowl, blend sour cream and molasses. In yet another bowl, blend flour, baking soda, ginger, and allspice. Add the molasses blend and the flour blend alternately into the butter-egg mix, mixing between each. Pour into two well-greased and floured 9-inch cake pans. Bake in preheated oven. Done when an inserted toothpick comes out dry.

Serve sliced with whipped cream or ice cream.

VARIATIONS
᷒ Fold in ½ cup raisins after all ingredients are mixed.
᷒ Substitute plain yogurt for the sour cream.

Molasses Cake

BAKING TIME: *30 minutes*
OVEN TEMPERATURE: *350 degrees*

> *2 cups all-purpose flour*
> *1 cup granulated sugar*
> *1 teaspoon baking powder*
> *1 teaspoon baking soda*
> *1 teaspoon salt*
> *½ cup solid shortening*
> *¾ cup milk*
> *1 teaspoon vanilla*
> *½ cup molasses*
> *2 eggs, beaten*

Blend flour, sugar, baking powder, baking soda, and salt in a large bowl. Add shortening, milk, and vanilla. Blend again; then beat at medium speed for 1 minute. Add the molasses, then the eggs one at a time, mixing between each addition. Pour mixture into two well-greased and floured 8-inch cake pans. Bake in preheated oven until cake begins to pull away from sides.

VARIATIONS
∾ Slice each cake in half to make four layers. Spread chunky applesauce between each layer, then top with powdered sugar.
∾ Try a cream cheese filling by beating two 8-ounce packages of softened cream cheese with 3 cups powdered sugar.

*I*n the Old West, despite its distinct and often tiresome flavor, molasses and its close cousin, sorghum, were particularity popular when used in cakes or other baked goods. They were the most inexpensive sweeteners and freely available.

Old West hands welcomed a cake like this, molasses-flavored or not, because of its departure from the ever present puddings that were much easier for cooks to prepare.

Here's a recipe using most of the ingredients available to ranch cooks. Its preparation is unusual by today's standards because of the order in which ingredients are added. It results in a coarsely textured cake, but is authentic.

Oatmeal Cake

BAKING TIME: *30–35 minutes*
OVEN TEMPERATURE: *350 degrees*

1 cup quick oats
1½ cups boiling water
1 cup brown sugar
1 cup granulated sugar
½ cup butter or margarine
2 eggs, beaten
1½ cups all-purpose flour
1 teaspoon baking powder
½ teaspoon cinnamon
¼ teaspoon ground cloves
1 teaspoon salt

Place all oats in a heat-proof bowl and pour boiling water over them. Let stand for 5 minutes. Set aside to cool. Cream sugars and butter until well blended. Mix in eggs and set aside. In a separate bowl, mix dry ingredients. Add slowly to sugar-butter mix, and when blended, add cooled oatmeal mix. When all is blended, pour into two well-greased and floured 8-inch cake pans. Place in preheated oven until toothpick or knife comes out dry when inserted into cake. Let set up for 5 minutes. Turn out and cool on wire rack.

Delicious with a butter cream frosting.

Historians state oats were once a weed that proved so hardy, it was better grown as a crop: not the most flattering past. Oats have been harvested in the colder climates of Europe for at least three thousand years. They're primarily used in cereals and breads, and if the consumer tires of the taste, they make excellent animal feed.

Like many other foods, what proved to be popular in Europe was also favored in the Old West. Oats filled the bill on a number of fronts. It was simple to grow, stored exceptionally well, was inexpensive, and tasted reasonably good. In the Old West, oats appeared in a number of mush recipes as a morning meal and easily supplemented other ingredients in puddings and breads.

This is an unusual recipe because oats are used in a cake. Oats add a hearty texture to the dessert dish. You won't be disappointed.

One-Egg Cake

BAKING TIME: *30 minutes*
OVEN TEMPERATURE: *350 degrees*

1 cup granulated sugar
½ cup butter or margarine
1 egg, beaten
1 teaspoon vanilla
2 cups all-purpose flour
½ teaspoon salt
1 teaspoon baking soda
1 teaspoon baking powder
1 cup buttermilk
1 cup raisins, chopped

Cream sugar and butter until light and fluffy. Add egg and vanilla; beat until blended. In a separate bowl, blend a dry mix of flour, salt, baking soda, and baking powder. Add buttermilk to the butter-sugar blend, alternating with the dry mix. Blend until well mixed, about 2–3 minutes. Fold in raisins and pour into 2 well-greased and floured 8-inch cake pans. Bake in preheated oven. Done when inserted toothpick comes out dry.

Delicious with a butter frosting.

VARIATIONS
∽ Frost with powdered sugar or lemon frosting.
∽ Cake will easily accept finely chopped nuts. Add about ½ cup with the raisins.

It didn't take long for pioneers to determine egg-laying chickens were very fragile creatures. Few birds survived the trip west. Cattle drive cooks had the same problem and concluded that chickens were obviously not designed to migrate in wagons. If by some miracle chickens did survive a move, they certainly did so without the bother of laying eggs.

However, the eggs proved a bit hardier than their parents. Carefully packing a number of raw eggs was a popular alternative to carrying along the uncooperative contributor of the product, but the eggs had to be preserved first. Pioneers used many innovative methods. The notion was simply to keep air off the shell to retard spoilage. Some eggs were dipped in paraffin, and others were stored in brine. Probably the most creative approach was to cover the egg in a hardy blend of borax. Borax boiled in water would adhere to the egg shell and crystallize around it, creating a seal.

This One-Egg Cake recipe is testimony to the possibilities when one is faced with limited resources. While its texture is coarse, the cake is delicious.

Sourdough Bread Cake

It may sound strange, but for centuries this was the most popular method to assemble a cake product. Leavening agents other than yeast were not really used until the late 1700s, so the cake products we know today were all made from the same starter as used in sourdough bread. Sourdough starter was found on every ranch, every wagon train, and every cattle drive. It was only natural to design a wonderful cake around it.

Few "yeast cakes" or "bread cakes" are made today because they are a bit chewier and harder to make than the baking powder variety. Here is an authentic recipe updated in two ways. The first technique uses a sourdough starter, and the second, if no starter is available, uses modern granulated yeast, a slight modification in ingredients.

The original recipe stated "spices to taste." There is no indication of what was used, but nutmeg and cinnamon were very popular, so they're included.

BAKING TIME: *30 minutes*
OVEN TEMPERATURE: *350 degrees*

1 cup sourdough starter
1 cup granulated sugar
½ cup butter or margarine
3 eggs
½ teaspoon cinnamon
½ teaspoon nutmeg
½ cup raisins
1 cup all-purpose flour
1 teaspoon baking soda
1 teaspoon baking powder

To make a sourdough starter see the chapter on bread (page 46–47). If you don't have a starter, use 1 cup warm water and 1 package of dry, powdered yeast.

Cream sugar and butter until light and fluffy. Add starter and mix thoroughly. Beat eggs, then blend in a little at a time. Add spices and raisins, and let it rise until light. In a separate bowl, blend flour, baking soda, and baking powder. Now add flour slowly while blending mix to make a tolerably stiff batter. Turn out into two well-greased and floured 9-inch cake pans. Bake in preheated oven. Done when inserted toothpick comes out dry.

This is not a delicate cake, so generous slices are best.

Railroad Cake

BAKING TIME: *30 minutes*

OVEN TEMPERATURE: *350 degrees*

> 1 cup granulated sugar
> ½ cup butter or margarine (1 stick)
> 2 eggs
> 2 cups all-purpose flour
> ½ teaspoon salt
> 2 teaspoons baking soda
> juice of 1 lemon
> 1 cup buttermilk
> 1 teaspoon salt

Cream sugar and butter until light and fluffy. Add eggs, blending well. In a separate bowl, combine flour, salt, and baking soda. Add to creamed mix slowly, alternating with lemon juice and buttermilk. When well blended, turn out into two 8-inch cake pans that have been well-greased and floured. Place in a preheated oven. Done when an inserted toothpick comes out dry.

A slice on a bed of hot cream is a nice touch of the Old West.

VARIATIONS

↪ Sprinkle with powdered sugar for a decorative look.

↪ Delete lemon and add 1 teaspoon almond extract for a nutty flavor.

↪ Slice in half lengthwise and frost with any of the icing recipes.

The source of this recipe was printed about the time the railroads came through the Old West. One can safely assume it must have been served in a dining car on at least one trip. Railroads not only brought new recipes to the West, but literally changed the face of the land as well. Whereas it would take four to six months to cross the country by wagon train, the railroad cut this trek to weeks.

Not much is recorded on railroad dining, but a few references refer to the limited bill of fare. This cake recipe reflects the need to keep it simple, but palatable. But one must remember, competition on the train was nonexistent, so there was little incentive to get creative. Some restaurants catered to passengers at fuel and water stops along the way, but quality was suspect since they never saw the same customer twice.

It is safe to assume that coach passengers carried nonperishable food to save precious dollars for their new settlement, but a slice of this railroad cake could have been a real treat and well worth the money.

Spice Cake

Tasty sugar was at a premium in the Old West. Near the end of the nineteenth century, the new railroad brought in refined sugar, but it was so expensive, few could afford the indulgence. Many pioneers heading West came from areas of the country where finding sweetening ingredients wasn't a problem. New England had maple sugar, the Deep South had sugar cane, and the Northeast had honey. As travelers moved westward, the foliage they used to draw their sugar became rare. A substitute had to be found.

Entering center stage was sorgo, or sorghum, with a flavor resembling cane sugar. The key word is "resembling," for its popularity was based solely on cost and availability. Virtually every ranch house and chuck wagon recipe calling for sugar used sorghum molasses. This wouldn't have been so terrible if the taste weren't so distinctive. It was almost impossible to get away from the flavor. The heavy use of spices as in this one hundred fifty-year-old Spice Cake recipe was one attempt to do so.

BAKING TIME: *45 minutes*
OVEN TEMPERATURE: *350 degrees*

1 cup granulated sugar
½ cup butter or margarine
3 eggs, beaten
½ cup molasses
½ cup milk
1 teaspoon baking soda
2 cups all-purpose flour
1 teaspoon cinnamon
½ teaspoon cloves
1 teaspoon allspice
1 teaspoon ginger
¼ teaspoon nutmeg
½ cup raisins

Cream sugar and butter until light and fluffy. Add eggs one at a time, mixing well. In a separate bowl, add molasses to milk and blend thoroughly. In yet one more bowl, blend baking soda, flour, and spices. Slowly add dry mix to sugar-butter-egg mixture, alternating with the milk and mixing constantly. Add raisins and mix thoroughly. Pour into a well-greased and floured bread pan and bake in a preheated oven. Done when inserted toothpick comes out dry.

Frost with a boiled icing and serve in hearty slices.

Spiced Sourdough Cake

BAKING TIME: *40 minutes*
OVEN TEMPERATURE: *325 degrees*

> *2 cups sourdough starter*
> *1 cup sugar*
> *4 eggs, beaten*
> *1 cup butter or margarine, melted*
> *1 teaspoon baking soda*
> *½ teaspoon cloves*
> *½ teaspoon allspice*
> *1 teaspoon cinnamon*
> *1–2 cups all-purpose flour*

To make a sourdough starter, see the chapter on bread (pages 46–47). Without a starter, use 2 cups warm water and 1 package of dry powdered yeast.

When sourdough is light and bubbly, add sugar. Mix together thoroughly and set in a warm spot to rise until very light. Depending on starter activity, 2–6 hours is typical. After the mixture is light and bubbly, stir in eggs, butter, baking soda, spices, and enough flour until batter is as stiff as a thick cake batter. Pour into two well-greased 8-inch cake pans or one large 9 x 15-inch pan, and bake in a preheated oven. Done when it springs back to the touch or when an inserted toothpick comes out dry.

Cut into big slices. Will keep 2–3 days like fresh bread.

Particularly easy to fix on the trail, bread cakes could take much more abuse in assembling and in baking than cakes made with baking soda or powder. Cakes made on the trail were very hearty and coarsely textured.

For baking, a small cake pan was inserted into a Dutch oven, and the Dutch oven lid was covered with hot embers. Pioneers also could easily modify one of the many portable stoves available. The small camp stoves were lightweight, inexpensive, and folded for traveling. They sat directly in the hot embers and heated rapidly. It's not clear how quickly they cooled for packing, so they probably made some baking or cooking impractical during rapid stopovers.

When making Spiced Sourdough Cake, use a ripe sourdough starter and ensure it is bubbling smartly before incorporating additional ingredients.

This recipe was also used as a base for a light fruit cake. Fold in two cups dried fruit before adding additional flour.

Tit-Tat-Toe Cake

Although this recipe is unusual enough to appear in modern cookbooks, it was developed a century and a half ago. It reflects the use of everyday ingredients in a unique way, typical of Old West bakers. Both raisins and currants were listed in the original recipe. Raisins were popular because they rarely spoiled, and wild grapes were everywhere. The use of currants reflected an Old World influence. Only raisins are used in this recipe, but feel free to add both.

The design in each slice must have thrilled the consumer. It's a nice display of colors and textures. One of the wonderful things about this cake is that it can be frosted with virtually any flavor to change its character.

This is a tall cake so small slices look smashing. Frost with butter cream or flavored boiled icing.

Pictured opposite, from top, are Tit-Tat-Toe Cake (this page) and Watermelon Cake (page 90).

BAKING TIME: *25–35 minutes*
OVEN TEMPERATURE: *350 degrees*

Base:
1 cup granulated sugar
½ cup butter or margarine
3 eggs, beaten
2 cups all-purpose flour
2 teaspoons baking powder
1 teaspoon salt
1 cup milk
Layer 1:
½ cup raisins
½ teaspoon cinnamon
½ teaspoon nutmeg
Layer 2:
2 tablespoons lemon extract
Layer 3:
2 tablespoons cocoa

Cream sugar and butter until light and fluffy. Add eggs; beat well, blending thoroughly. In a separate bowl, mix flour, baking powder, and salt. Add in thirds to sugar-butter mix, alternating with milk and blending between each addition. When blended, divide mix into three equal parts (about 1⅓ cups per layer). Season layers as indicated. Turn into three well-greased and floured 8-inch cake pans, and bake in a preheated oven. Done when toothpick inserted into cake comes out dry.

Watermelon Cake

It wasn't possible to get too creative with exotic ingredients while on the Plains. Even if the goods were available, most were far too expensive for something as frivolous as a cake. Here, an enterprising baker used standard ingredients to create a cake of interest. It comes in two colors, and raisins are added to represent seeds. Watermelon cake appears in more than one old recipe book, so it must have been a reasonably popular item. Because it was awhile before real watermelon appeared in the Old West in any numbers, this cake may have been a way to reflect on memories of an easier time back home.

The texture is authentically coarse due to the absence of eggs, but it doesn't affect the flavor.

BAKING TIME: *40 minutes*
OVEN TEMPERATURE: *350 degrees*

> *1 cup granulated sugar*
> *½ cup butter or margarine*
> *1 cup milk*
> *2 teaspoons baking powder*
> *½ teaspoon salt*
> *2 cups all-purpose flour*
> *1 teaspoon lemon or orange bits*
> *red food coloring*

Cream sugar and butter until well mixed. Add milk and mix well for at least 2 minutes at medium-high speed. In a separate bowl, blend baking powder, salt, and flour. Add to sugar mix, slowly mixing all the while. Fold in lemon or orange bits. Now separate batter into two bowls and set one aside. In the second bowl add a few drops of red food coloring. Mix and add until a nice pink color appears. Now fold in raisins to the pink-colored mixture. Grease and flour two 8-inch cake pans. Pour half the white batter around the outside edge of each of the cake pans. Pour the pink batter in the middle of each pan. Tap the pans lightly to ensure the colors merge and bake in a preheated oven.

VARIATION
∽ For additional flavor add a teaspoon of vanilla extract.

Western Fruit Cake

BAKING TIME: *1 hour or more*
OVEN TEMPERATURE: *375 degrees*

1 cup granulated sugar
1½ cups water
1 cup raisins
½ cup solid shortening
1 cup all-purpose flour
1 cup whole wheat flour
2 teaspoons baking powder
½ teaspoon salt
1 teaspoon nutmeg
1 teaspoon cinnamon

Boil sugar, water, and raisins together for 3 minutes. While cooling, cut in shortening and flours in a separate bowl until mealy and coarse. Then add baking powder, salt, nutmeg, and cinnamon to shortening mix. Blend well; then pour into sugar mix and stir until completely blended. Pour into well-greased 7-inch loaf pans and place in a preheated oven. Done when inserted toothpick comes out dry.

Lasts a long time. Serve sliced thin.

VARIATIONS
∽ Use ¼ cup of any kind of dried fruit with the raisins.
∽ Add ¼ cup chopped nuts with the spices.

Virtually all edible fruits can be dried, cured, and eaten later. For hundreds of years, Native Americans prepared dried fruits by mashing fruit between two good-size rocks, then storing it for later use. As their techniques evolved, they used specialized stones. Although the American Indian mano (hand stone) and metate (base stone) were generally thought of as grinding stones for corn flour, their use was in fact far wider.

Native Americans often ground wild plums, chokeberries, gooseberries, and more with these stones—pits and all. The result was molded into small thin cakes and dried, not baked. This "pemomican," or fruit cake, could be eaten immediately or saved. It kept exceptionally well and must have made a splendid traveling companion.

Don't expect to see one in your birthday basket; few are made any longer. However, a delicious alternative is this Western Fruit Cake blended from three Old West recipes. It has a coarser texture than found in many of today's perennial Christmas varieties, but is delicious.

ARBUCKLE'S:
THE COFFEE OF THE WEST

The Arbuckle Coffee Company was started in 1859 by three men bent on making coffee a fixture in every home. Until the Arbuckles, customers outside major cities could buy only green coffee beans. Roasting was done in the unskilled hands of the kitchen cook. As expected, quality varied widely—usually from dismal to ghastly.

John Arbuckle proceeded to apply a scientific approach to roasting and preserving the quality of coffee beans to enable shipping anywhere, preroasted.

In 1868 he patented his process and began manufacturing, much to the scoffs and laughter of his competitors. This process was heavily marketed under the name Ariosa, the meaning of which was never revealed. To give it a boost over its more familiar competitors, premiums were offered to purchasers and local customers. Everything from suspenders to laundry wringers were available for just a few coupons.

Over the next forty years, Arbuckle ground every competitor finer than his coffee. Ariosa was virtually the only coffee known west of the Mississippi. From campfires to range homes, Arbuckle's was the coffee of choice.

By the time John Arbuckle died in 1912, his empire was worth over $33 million—in early 1900, dollars that probably would have bought the state of Arizona.

Icings: Historic Toppings

T HE KEY TO ASSEMBLING CENTURY-OLD TOPPING RECIPES IS simplicity. Flavorings, while creative, were limited, but great things could be done with little.

One of the most popular Old West techniques was dusting the top with fine powdered sugar. The hardest work was grinding the block sugar to a fine powder before it would stick to the cake. Today it's just a matter of pulling the right box off the grocery shelves. Boiled icings were also in fashion at ranch houses because of low cost and long-keeping properties. They are very different from today's creamy varieties.

Presented here is a mix of old and new. Like the cake recipes, old recipes are adjusted to mix in modern kitchens, but the taste and texture of the old is still apparent. Few decoration hints were ever provided; apparently, it was a magnificent treat for ranch hands just to get a cake with icing.

Kitchens of the Old West used whatever and wherever available to finish the cake. Wagon seats or keg tops were favorite spots. From there, the cake could sit on an old flour sack and be turned in any direction. Later, for clean up, the same flour sack served as a dish towel.

In today's kitchens, if it's possible to place the cake on a turning stand, the job is considerably easier, but if none is available, place the cake on a piece of waxed paper to turn. Finish the task by carefully setting the cake onto the serving tray and lifting a corner of the cake to remove the paper. Another method of turning is to place the cake on folded strips of aluminum foil. The cake can be rotated and lifted onto a serving tray easily, and the strips can be removed just by sliding them out.

As a general rule, use about one-fourth of the icing between layers. It's easiest to start on the top of the cake and work the icing down over the sides.

(continued on page 95)

HUMOR ON THE RANGE

Despite eighteen-hour work days, cattle drives and ranch work were not with-out their lighter moments. However, the humor was a bit more brash than one would encounter today.

The originator of many practical jokes was the cook. One could assume he was the one who could get away with it, at least if the butt of the joke ever wanted to eat again. Since the cook was usually first up in the morning, presumably to fix breakfast, it was an ideal time for a practical joke or two. Tying a sleeping cowboy's feet to a log and ringing loudly for breakfast always satisfied the prankster's darker side. Smearing raw bread dough into a cowpoke's hair while he lay in deep sleep provided great entertainment for the rest of the group.

Sometimes it went beyond good taste, literally.

Easy Boiled Icing

4 egg whites
2 cups granulated sugar
¼ teaspoon salt
¼ cup water
3 tablespoons light corn syrup
¼ teaspoon cream of tartar

Mix egg whites, sugar, salt, and water in a bowl. Mix well, then blend in corn syrup and cream of tartar. Use a double boiler. If none is available, use a heatproof glass bowl or stainless steel bowl inserted on top of a pan half-filled with simmering water. Place bowl on top of steam heat and beat the mixture immediately for 6–8 minutes until it becomes stiff and peaks when beater is lifted. Flavorings can be mixed in when cool.

FLAVORING VARIATIONS
Add all flavorings slowly, beating all the while, after the frosting is cooked.
꠲ Vanilla: Add 1 teaspoon vanilla extract.
꠲ Tangy: Add 1 tablespoon fresh orange or lemon bits.
꠲ Almond: Add 1 teaspoon almond extract.
꠲ Chocolate: Melt 3 small blocks semi-sweet chocolate in 1 tablespoon butter. Fold in carefully.
꠲ Liqueur: Add 1 tablespoon, or more, of a favorite.

Old-Fashioned Boiled Icing

Sugar syrup:
> 2 cups sugar
> 1 cup water

Icing:
> 3 egg whites, beaten to peaked stage
> ¼ teaspoon cream of tartar

In a saucepan, blend sugar and water with a whisk. Turn heat to medium hot and stir mixture until it boils. When it starts boiling and mixture reaches 240 degrees (on a candy thermometer), stop stirring. Let it cool slightly, then pour a steady, thin stream into egg whites, beating all the while. When icing is thick, add cream of tartar and any flavoring desired.

If the mix does not thicken, cook over a double boiler or pot of simmering water. If it gets too hard, add a tablespoon of hot water to the mix and blend.

FLAVORING VARIATIONS

Add all flavorings slowly, beating all the while, after the frosting is cooked.

⌐ Vanilla: Add 1 teaspoon vanilla extract.

⌐ Tangy: Add 1 tablespoon fresh orange or lemon bits.

⌐ Almond: Add 1 teaspoon almond extract.

⌐ Liqueur: Add 1 tablespoon, or more, of a favorite.

Feeling especially cantankerous, the cook's most delectable-appearing dessert could be made with dirt or scrub brush. This brought a deep laugh from the instigator, with few consequences.

What usually kept the cowboy from crippling his tormentor would be the unwritten law of replacement. A cowboy who criticized, wounded, or maimed the cook had to do all the cooking himself until the cook's pride returned or time healed his injury. Certainly one dare not kill him; the finality of it all was too much.

COOKBOOKS: NOT FOR EVERYONE

Although we can't imagine even the most basic kitchen without a cookbook or two, few existed in the Old West. This was due not to the lack of printing facilities, but to the low literacy rate. Few could read, so why waste valuable space and dollars on something never used.

Those who could read had a different set of problems. Most cookbooks available during this period were European with European measurements. In American fashion, we developed our own gauge that everyone could understand. A cup, a teaspoon, and a tablespoon were utensils all had on hand, even out on the open range. They became standards we still use today.

Butter Cream Frosting

*4 cups powdered sugar
1 cup softened unsalted butter
4 tablespoons water
1 teaspoon vanilla*

Beat all ingredients together until light. If it's too thick, add more water. If it's too thin, add more sugar.

FLAVORING VARIATIONS
Add all flavorings after the frosting ingredients are beaten together.
⁓ Tangy: Add 1 tablespoon fresh orange or lemon bits.
⁓ Coffee: Add 1 teaspoon instant coffee.
⁓ Almond: Add 1 teaspoon almond extract, delete vanilla.
⁓ Coconut: Add ½ cup coconut flakes.
⁓ Peanut: Add ½ cup peanut butter, smooth or crunchy.
⁓ Chocolate: Melt 3 small blocks semisweet chocolate in 1 tablespoon butter.

Jelly Glaze

2 cups jelly

Melt jelly and cook down slightly. Immediately pour over fresh cake.

FLAVORING VARIATION
〜 Add 1 tablespoon, or more, of a favorite liqueur, after the jelly is melted and cooked down.

Meringue

4 egg whites
½ cup powdered sugar
¼ teaspoon cream of tartar

Beat together until peaks form when beaters are removed. Spread over cake (or pie) and place in preheated oven at 350 degrees for 5–8 minutes, until meringue is golden brown around the edges.

ROTARY EGG BEATERS

When the first Dover Standard Company Rotary Egg Beater was patented on May 31, 1870, one hundred forty egg beater patents followed.

However, as advertised by the leading egg beater company, the Dover is "the most effective Egg Beater made. Held in the hand with an immovable rest, it stands firmly wherever placed and will beat eggs with greater rapidity than any other."

PORCELAIN ENAMEL

Porcelain enamel is ironware coated with a high-fired, glasslike composition. It was invented and subsequently applied to saucepans by Dr. Hinkling in 1799. It was later refined and applied to other kinds of kitchenware by 1839.

Probably more than any other coating process developed for cookware, enamel coating raised the ire of all other manufacturers of pots and pans. Porcelain enamel was accused of causing physical ailments from appendicitis to food poisoning. The battle raged into the early 1900s. When the scientific community finally caught up with the development of new materials, it proved once and for all that "never has any intestinal disturbance been found to have originated from . . . enamel." Good news after one hundred years of use.

However, this didn't stop the debate on quality. As reported by the New York Times, *March 1890, "Domestic enameled ironware is not very durable, the base being of iron . . . and nearly all foreign ware is in blue and white, and is more attractive than the mottled graniteware of the American producers."*

Nonetheless, pieces of porcelain enamel are still used in kitchens today— without intestinal discomfort, I might add.

Pioneer Pies
and Cobblers

*John W. Powell, F. E. Colbourn, Thomas Moran,
and Jacob Hamblin, 1873.*

Pies and Other Delectables

"AS AMERICAN AS APPLE PIE" SHOWS WHAT STATUS WE PLACE ON this simple dish. Virtually every region of the country has its own claim to pie fame, and western pioneers brought much of that with them. On the way west they incorporated indigenous products to create new, wonderful pies.

Pies are hardly a new food. Recorded history details pie recipes at least two thousand years old. Egyptians, Romans, and Greeks had versions of pies, but it was the Europeans who brought them to an art form, literally. European banquet tables were rarely without some form of pie. Competing chefs made pies and their contents as enticing and unusual as possible. Virtually nothing was immune to enclosure in a pastry shell, from live birds to swimming fish. Fortunately, someone moved the competition into a more palatable arena and included sweeter contents. As the pastry made its way to the New World, our prolific fruit was used to fill pie shells to create desserts.

Pie shapes never appeared as an issue until the sixteenth century. Until then, pies appeared in a variety of containers, and few were round—at least until American colonists got hold of them. As the story goes, in colonial days, when supplies were scarce, pies were made circular to "cut corners." The result was so attractive, easy to slice, and simple to bake that it stuck. Stretching the food dollar never had such a delectable result.

In the pioneeers' trek west, pie recipes went along for the ride. Fruit pies were always popular, but seasonal, so alternatives for year-round combinations were developed. What we now consider unusual mixtures were commonplace. Two of the most popular year-round pies were vinegar pie and sweet potato pie. They were a tradition among ranch hands, pioneers, and cowboys on cattle drives.

Pictured from top are Raisin Pie (page 114) and Apple Crumb Cobbler (page 107).

Ingredients were readily available and easily sweetened. One can't possibly imagine what a fresh pie must have smelled like to a cowhand meandering in after fourteen hours of cow-punching.

The recipes for most of the following pies are over one hundred years old. They also present unusual blends that perhaps you haven't tried before. (A few basic pie crust recipes are found at the end of the chapter.)

MOCK APPLE PIE

With packing space at a premium on wagons heading west, only essentials were loaded. Foodstuffs were purchased or picked enroute.

It is not difficult to imagine the homesickness after just a few months on the trail. Even the simplest tasks and most basic foods took on new meaning. Pies were a perennial favorite with pioneers, but ingredients weren't as convenient as before, so new favorites took their place, such as vinegar pie or sweet potato pie. Many always came back to popular apple pie, though.

Dried apples solved some of the problems for those who could afford the cost or storage space. For those who couldn't, mock apple pie was created. Many older recipe books and personal journals refer to this pretender, so it must have been a good answer to the craving. One writer stated: "The deception was most complete and readily accepted. Apples at this early date were a dollar a pound and we young people all craved a piece of mother's apple pie to appease our home sick feelings."

Mock apple pie is easily reproduced today; however, you must be willing to bake your own crackers. The soda crackers in the Old West were considerably more substantial than today's airy variety. Cracker recipes appear on pages 164 and 165. The only changes you must make are to roll the cracker dough out to ¼–½ inch thick and to bake twice as long.

From Mrs. Cronkite's Cook Book, *published in the 1800s: "Baking time: Break four large soda crackers into an earthen bowl. Pour over them a pint of cold water, made very tart with citric acid. When soft, but not mashed, removed the soda crackers to your pie plate with the under crust already on; then sift over, 2 tablespoons of light brown sugar and a little allspice and cinnamon to flavor the brown sugar and give the requisite color, after which put on a prettily perforated top crust and bake in a very quick oven a few moments."*

Grated Apple–Raspberry Pie

BAKING TIME: *45–55 minutes*
OVEN TEMPERATURE: *375 degrees*

1 cup raspberries (1 pint)
5 large peeled, tart apples
1 cup sugar
⅛ teaspoon salt
1 teaspoon lemon juice
2 tablespoons cornstarch

Rinse the raspberries well and place into a large bowl. Grate the apples, with a cheese grater or a food processor. They should equal 3–4 cups of apples. Combine with the raspberries; add sugar, salt, lemon juice, and cornstarch and mix well. Pour into a prepared pie shell, spread evenly, and add a pie pastry top. Bake until bubbly, about 50 minutes.

Warm, this is sinfully delicious. Á la mode comes in a close second.

VARIATIONS

ↄ It is possible to substitute strawberries; however, cut them to the size of raspberries to ensure the flavor is spread throughout the pie.

ↄ For nut fanatics, walnuts or pecans mix nicely. Add ½–¾ cup with the fruit before pouring into the pie shell.

ↄ This is one of those pies that is extremely attractive with a lattice top.

Berries were not an unusual find on the plains. A treat for both Native American and cowboy alike, few berries made it from the vine to the baker's table without being consumed by the collectors.

The most popular were chokecherries, elderberries, hackberries, and wolfberries. Unfortunately, some of these had to be cooked before consumption to bring out the true sweet flavor. That didn't seem to bother many hungry gatherers.

For those exhibiting enough self-discipline to share their bounty, all sorts of creative possibilities existed. Berries were mashed and added to breads and biscuits, and others would find their way into a variety of sweet desserts.

For more contemporary bakers, most Old West berries are not generally found at the corner store, so raspberries are substituted. The taste is not far from that created by a week's worth of gathering, cooking, and mashing wild varieties.

The lineage of buttermilk pies is dubious. Supposedly created in the Deep South, it appeared throughout the West in cookbooks and personal journals. All ingredients were available to ranch house cooks. However, on the range, milk was a rare commodity, so a cowboy working a cattle drive would have to wait until they passed a ranch with a generous owner, or go to town.

Originally, buttermilk was the residue left after churning milk for butter. Little was wasted in Old West kitchens, so buttermilk was used as an excellent catalyst for creative endeavors, and the natural cultures growing in milk gave it a distinct flavor to mix with both old and new recipes. Today, buttermilk is made from pasteurized skim milk and tightly controlled cultures. It's not nearly as tasty, but far safer.

Buttermilk Pie is a rich, sweet dessert that has to be tried to be believed.

Buttermilk Pie

BAKING TIME: *40–60 minutes*
OVEN TEMPERATURE: *375 degrees*

> *1 cup granulated sugar*
> *¼ teaspoon salt*
> *¼ cup all-purpose flour*
> *3 eggs*
> *1 cup buttermilk*
> *1 teaspoon vanilla*
> *½ cup butter or margarine, melted*

Mix sugar, salt, and flour and set aside. In another bowl, beat eggs. Add buttermilk, vanilla, and butter to eggs; then add all to dry ingredients and mix well. Pour into an unbaked 8-inch pie shell. Bake for 40–60 minutes until golden brown. Pie will rise or "puff" up in the oven and fall again when cool. This is normal.

Serve cold. Best if allowed to set up at least 6 hours in a refrigerator.

VARIATIONS
↝ Add a meringue topping for a truly spectacular appearance.
↝ If you like raisins, this recipe lends itself well to ½ cup of raisins added to the mix just before pouring into the pie shell. Most will settle, but who cares.
↝ For fun, you can add food coloring, a nice touch for the holidays.

Butterscotch Pie

BAKING TIME: *none*

1 cup light brown sugar
3 tablespoons all-purpose flour
4 teaspoon cornstarch
¼ teaspoon salt
1½ cups whole milk
3 eggs (separated)
4 tablespoons butter or margarine
1 teaspoon vanilla

Bake a pie crust in an 8-inch pie pan.

Blend brown sugar, flour, cornstarch, and a pinch of salt in a bowl. Pour in half the milk and mix until smooth. Heat mix with remaining milk in one of two ways: in a double boiler or directly on top of the stove on very low heat. With either method, stir constantly until thickened, about 15 minutes. Beat the egg yolks thoroughly. Add a bit of the hot mix to the eggs; then pour the eggs into the hot mix, stirring and cooking for another 3–4 minutes. Add butter and vanilla, and stir in until butter is melted. Beat egg whites until nice and stiff. Fold into hot mixture and stir lightly to blend; then pour into baked pie shell. It will set up on the kitchen shelf or faster in the refrigerator.

VARIATION

∽ Add ½ cup raisins or finely chopped walnuts just before adding egg whites.

Although Butterscotch Pie may sound strange, it is a tasty combination of popular ingredients poured into a pie dish. It may have originated in the Deep South; but no matter, recipes from all over the world wound up on the ranch hand's table in the Old West. Difficult to prepare on the back of a chuck wagon, it was a snap on the larger ranches with the luxury of a stove.

Cobblers were a popular diversion from other sweets and easy to make. It wasn't uncommon for a chuck wagon cook to reward a particularly helpful cowpoke with a cobbler made just for him. While this tasty treat for one didn't endear the cowboy to his peers, it assured even tighter command by the master of meals.

Cobblers come in many forms. Some parts of the country call them deep dish pies. Others cover the fruit with a pastry crust and sprinkle the top with sugar. Although there is little recorded on which version the plains' cooks preferred, place your bets on the easiest variety; a biscuit mix poured over fruit and baked.

In deference to modern tastes, some ingredients have been changed to keep the dish within reason. Some western ingredients used on the open range are just as well left alone.

Cherry-Cherry Cobbler

BAKING TIME: *40–50 minutes*
OVEN TEMPERATURE: *375 degrees*

> ½ cup soft butter or margarine
> 1 cup granulated sugar
> 1 egg
> 1 cup all-purpose flour
> 1 teaspoon baking powder
> ½ cup milk
> 1 can cherry pie filling

Cut butter into small pieces (set aside 1 tablespoon to grease baking dish), and mix with sugar. Beat in egg. Blend flour and baking powder together in separate bowl; then, alternating with milk, add to other mixture and mix lightly. Grease a 9-inch dish or cake pan with leftover butter and pour in pie filling. Drop biscuit mix by tablespoonfuls on top of cherries and place uncovered in a preheated oven to bake. Top should be golden brown and the fruit bubbling.

Given time to set up, it will still be messy to serve. Just relax, that's part of the charm. Top with fresh cream, whipped cream, or vanilla ice cream.

VARIATION
↝ This is a fruit cobbler, so substitution is simple. Pie fillings are the easiest to use, although canned peaches will work. Drain the juice off any canned fruit before use.

Apple Crumb Cobbler

BAKING TIME: *30 minutes*
OVEN TEMPERATURE: *375 degrees*

    5 large apples
    ¼ cup all-purpose flour
    1 cup brown sugar
    2 tablespoons granulated sugar
    ¼ teaspoon salt
    1 teaspoon cinnamon
    ¼ teaspoon nutmeg
    ½ cup dry bread crumbs
    ½ cup butter or margarine
    1 teaspoon lemon juice

Also called Old Apple Crisp or Apple Brown Betty, this has been an extremely popular dessert since the days of the first settlers. The recipe was taken west and modified a bit with molasses and fewer spices to accommodate rugged conditions. It baked up nicely in a Dutch oven and kept for a number of meals. This recipe is closer to the original intent of its creator.

Core, peel, and cut each apple into 16 wedges and set aside. Mix flour, sugars, salt, cinnamon, and nutmeg in a large bowl. Pour onto apples and mix so all are covered. Let sit until juice begins to form. Place bread crumbs in another bowl and cut in butter. Pour apple mix into well-buttered 9-inch baking dish. Sprinkle with lemon juice. Place butter mix on top, and cover with aluminum foil and bake for 30 minutes or until bubbly and apples are tender. For a crispy top, turn the oven to 400 degrees after the pie's done, and bake another 10 minutes.

    Unbelievable under a large scoop of French Vanilla ice cream or a bed of heavy cream.

For the first few weeks of each wagon train movement, fresh milk was abundant. Accompanying cows served the groups well, and numerous milk product recipes were made and enjoyed.

Spirits were high, and food was good. However, since food blends became simpler as road weary pioneers settled into a routine, this Cream Pie was most likely made only within the first few weeks of their trek. Cream was much harder to come by later in the trip. Cows either died en route or were slaughtered for meat as supplies dwindled.

When pioneers reached their destination, cows were once again plentiful, and Cream Pie was a popular dessert at ranch houses. It was made by incorporating fruits grown in the area and remains famous today as banana or chocolate cream pie.

This is the basic starter for most cream pies, so enjoy an updated recipe of a real cream pie so popular one hundred fifty years ago.

Cream Pie

BAKING TIME: *none*

2 cups whole milk
2 cups heavy whipping cream
1 cup powdered sugar
2 tablespoons all-purpose flour
2 teaspoons vanilla
½ teaspoon salt
4 egg yolks
1 tablespoon butter or margarine

Reserve ¼ cup milk. Pour cream and remaining milk into a large saucepan and cook over medium heat. Stir in powdered sugar. To reserved milk, add flour, vanilla, and salt; mix well. Pour into the saucepan. Whisk in egg yolks, add butter, and cook until thick, about 10–15 minutes. Pour into prebaked 9-inch pie shell and cool.

Slice and serve cool, not cold. Keeps well for 3 days.

VARIATIONS

꒜ For meringue topping, use remaining 4 egg whites. Add ¼ teaspoon cream of tartar and ½ cup powdered sugar; beat until peaks form. Spoon on carefully, and bake at 350 degrees for 10 minutes or until nicely browned.

꒜ Add sliced bananas to pie shell and pour cream mix over top.

꒜ Add 1 cup grated coconut to mix before pouring into shell.

Green Tomato Pie

BAKING TIME: *1 hour*
OVEN TEMPERATURE: *375 degrees*

> 8 peeled green tomatoes (medium)
> 1 tablespoon lemon juice
> 1 cup granulated sugar
> ¼ cup all-purpose flour
> ¼ teaspoon salt
> 1 teaspoon cinnamon
> ¼ teaspoon nutmeg

To peel the tomatoes, immerse them in boiling water until the skin becomes loose, about 2–3 minutes per tomato. Let them cool, and the skin should peel off easily with vegetable peeler. Slice the tomatoes into about ⅛-inch slices and place into a large bowl with lemon juice. In a separate bowl, blend together the sugar, flour, salt, cinnamon, and nutmeg. Pour this mix over the tomato slices and toss until slices are covered. Let stand about 5–10 minutes; then pour into prepared pie shell (unbaked). Place in a preheated oven for about 1 hour.

VARIATIONS
↩ For an even more interesting mix, delete the granulated sugar and substitute ¾ cup brown sugar.
↩ To change the texture, change the sugar as above and use 2 sliced and peeled apples. Reduce the green tomatoes to only 3.

Nesters" settled the entire West, staking their land and dreams on persistence and skills. Gathering food for a meal was no easy task. Visiting the corner grocery store often took an entire day, so the shopping list included mostly non-perishable necessities. Other needs were made, grown, or done without.

Ranch and open range dishes included unusual combinations of available ingredients. The home-grown garden was a favorite for such creativity. Here's a tasty and unusual combination, updated for our use. Be sure to use green tomatoes; if they are ripened, it's quite a mess and tastes entirely different.

Ice Cream Pie

espite its engaging name; it has nothing to do with ice cream except in appearance, but it helped pioneers satisfy a sorely missed treat.

Ice cream was gaining its astounding popularity during the time of the pioneers largest migration west. Developed and manufactured on the industrialized East Coast, ice cream could be served year-round. Unfortunately, Old West immigrants found many items taken for granted back home were simply impossible to obtain in the primitive West. With few industries in the West able to provide even the crudest refrigeration, ice cream was hopeless until the arrival of winter storms, and this was certainly not an ideal time to enjoy it.

Ice Cream Pie was probably designed to remind one of a huge scoop of good ice cream. The color of the pie was similar to vanilla, the most popular flavor of the day. Ice Cream Pie is a close cousin to cream pies and makes a terrific vanilla meringue pie. It will readily accept other flavorings, but is best just left with a plain vanilla ice cream taste.

BAKING TIME: *none*

   3 egg yolks
   3 tablespoons granulated sugar
   2 tablespoon cornstarch
   ½ teaspoon salt
   3 cups milk
   1 teaspoon vanilla

In a saucepan, mix egg yolks, sugar, cornstarch, and salt. Add milk and bring to a boil. Cook for 10–15 minutes or until thickened. Add vanilla. Pour thickened filling into prebaked 8-inch pie crust. Refrigerate for 2–3 hours until firm.

Serve the colder the better to simulate ice cream.

VARIATIONS

∽ Will easily adapt to other cream pie recipes. Add fresh fruit of your choice by lining the baked pie shell then pouring in mix.

Oatmeal–Black Walnut Pie

BAKING TIME: *45–50 minutes*
OVEN TEMPERATURE: *350 degrees*

> *1 ¼ cups quick oats*
> *1 ¼ cups chopped walnuts*
> *½ cup raisins*
> *4 tablespoons melted butter*
> *3 eggs, beaten*
> *½ cup sugar*
> *½ cup molasses*
> *1 teaspoon cinnamon*
> *¼ teaspoon salt*

In one bowl, mix oats, walnuts, raisins, and butter. Blend well. In another bowl, mix eggs, sugar, molasses, cinnamon, and salt. Mix both together and pour into a prepared (unbaked) 9-inch pie shell and even it out so the top is smooth. Place in a preheated oven for 45–50 minutes. For an untrained eye, it may be difficult to tell when the pie is done. One test is to jiggle the pie shell. When the top is slightly solidified, it's ready. Another method is to watch the edges. When the edges have risen and are brown, it is set to come out.

VARIATIONS
↩ This pie lends itself well to ¼ teaspoon nutmeg added with the cinnamon.
↩ Orange or lemon peel adds a zip to the sweet flavor. Add 1 teaspoon with the cinnamon.

*B*lack walnuts are found in Arizona and New Mexico. Extraordinarily prolific, they contain little meat, but what is available is delicious. Pioneers quickly learned from the Apache what a delicacy black walnuts are. Apaches used black walnuts not only in cooking and baking, but also in making a wonderful brown dye. They also employed it as a medicine for rheumatism or leg pains.

If black walnuts don't currently fill your pantry shelves, regular eastern walnuts work nicely and won't turn your fingers an unpleasant color.

This is a wonderful pie, truly different and easily assembled.

Orange Meringue Pie

One might reasonably ask what an Orange Pie recipe is doing in a book on the Old West. Although California attracted thousands of gold miners, it also attracted some of the most creative entrepreneurs in history. All were out to make their fortune, and each had an idea. William Wolfson was one such man.

Believed to have first been brought from Hawaii, small orange trees grew wild on the grounds of California missions. Wolfson saw an opportunity and in the mid-1800s took cuttings from a San Gabriel mission to grow his first orchard. This proved so successful that he expanded his orchards to include apricots, oranges, lemons, and figs. By the 1870s California had over forty-five thousand citrus trees, two-thirds of them Wolfson's. By 1877, he was shipping the fruit by railroad back East, and an industry was born.

This pie represented one of the newly found uses for oranges.

Pictured opposite, from top, are Wild Grape–Apple Pie (page 122) and Orange Meringue Pie (this page).

BAKING TIME: *7–10 minutes*
OVEN TEMPERATURE: *375 degrees*

Pie filling:
   3 tablespoons all-purpose flour
   ¼ cup cornstarch
   1 cup granulated sugar
   ¼ teaspoon salt
   1½ cups orange juice
   1 cup water
   4 egg yolks
   2 teaspoons butter
   Grated rind of 2 oranges
Meringue:
   4 egg whites
   ¼ teaspoon cream of tartar
   ½ cup powdered sugar

Combine flour, cornstarch, sugar, and salt in a medium pot. Add juice and water; keep stirring. Bring to boil. Boil for 2 minutes, stirring occasionally. Remove from heat. To egg yolks, add 1 cup of juice mixture from pan. Mix well and return it to the rest of mixture to cook until thickened, about 3–5 minutes. Add butter and orange rind. Let cool slightly. Beat egg whites with meringue ingredients until forming peaks. Pour filling into prebaked pie shell. Cover with meringue and bake until lightly browned, about 7–10 minutes.

Let the pie set up for at least an hour. Refrigerate and serve cool.

Raisin Pie

Wild grapes were abundant in the Southwest. With the popularity and versatility of dried fruits, dried grapes stood out as one of the more popular sweetening ingredients in pioneer and Native American foods. Drying the indigenous grape was easily done in the warm sun, no matter where the cook set up camp. They stored well and took up little room—a small sacrifice made for the intense flavor and sugar content. Also, no doubt raisins were one of the most frequent snacks for a tired cowboy on an all-night watch for coyotes and the like.

The proliferation of raisin dishes was natural. The fruit was added to numerous foods, but raisin pie was one of the more welcomed treats.

This is a wonderfully sweet recipe, perfect for a winter dessert.

BAKING TIME: *15–25 minutes*
OVEN TEMPERATURE: *425 degrees*

2 cups water
½ cup sugar
¼ cup dark corn syrup
¼ teaspoon salt
¼ teaspoon cinnamon
⅛ teaspoon nutmeg
⅛ teaspoon ginger
2 cups seedless raisins
4 tablespoons cornstarch
1 tablespoon lemon juice
3 teaspoons butter or margarine

In a saucepan, combine water, sugar, corn syrup, salt, cinnamon, nutmeg, and ginger. Bring to boil; lower heat to simmer and carefully add the raisins. Continue to cook for about 20 minutes. With about 2–3 tablespoons of water, blend the cornstarch to a mash and add slowly to the hot raisin mix. Cook for another 5 minutes. Add lemon juice and butter; then pour mix into a bowl to cool. When cool to the touch, pour into an uncooked pie shell and bake for 15–25 minutes. It's done when crust is brown.

Cool and let pie set up. It's even better the second day topped with ice cream or whipped cream.

(continued on following page)

VARIATIONS

∽ For a zing, substitute ½ cup of orange juice for ½ cup water.

∽ If you like nuts, ½ cup walnuts added with the cornstarch works nicely.

∽ An unusual texture can be had by running the cooled, cooked mix through a food processor for about 10–20 seconds. Pour into prepared pie shell and bake as before.

FRUITS AND STUFF

Aside from the heat, mid to late summer was a great time for bakers. The desert and high plains were alive with berries and fruit. Strawberries, raspberries, chokeberries, wolfberries, and mulberries were abundant. All but strawberries could be crushed, dried, and molded into fruit cakes. Berries were added to many recipes—some of renown, some better forgotten.

The most popular, wild grapes, presented wonderful opportunities for creative efforts. Native Americans taught early settlers how to dry them for raisins, which stored well and could be used throughout the year.

Wild apples, plums, and other tree fruits were also in abundance and used in a number of recipes, many of which are included here.

Although the Pennsylvania Dutch have laid claim to this popular dessert, it was often fixed on the open range as a breakfast dish. Sometimes called a molasses cake, its popularity was understandable. Ingredients were on hand, assembly was easy, and varieties abounded. The chuck wagon cook could be the day's hero by quickly throwing together basic goods and serving it piping hot, either as a pie or smaller pastry.

There are two schools of thought on preparation. The East Coast version used huge amounts of butter. With few dairy products available on the open range, cooks of the West preferred lard. There is a simple compromise—solid vegetable shortening. It keeps the crust from getting soggy and cuts down on cholesterol.

Southwest Shoofly Pie

BAKING TIME: *45 minutes*
OVEN TEMPERATURE: *375 degrees*

> *2 cups all-purpose flour*
> *½ cup granulated sugar*
> *½ cup solid shortening*
> *1 cup light molasses*
> *1 teaspoon baking soda*
> *1 cup boiling water*

Mix flour, sugar, and shortening. Blend with a pastry knife or quickly in a food processor until crumbly like oatmeal. Place the crumbly mix in a greased pie pan, and spread evenly on the bottom and up the sides, being careful not to compress the mix. Now blend molasses, baking soda, and boiling water; carefully pour over the crumbs. Bake in a preheated oven for 45 minutes. Sides will be slightly puffy when done.

Cool before serving and slice like a pie. If it breaks apart, or you desire variety, scoop out and serve in a dish topped with whipped cream. No one will ever know the difference.

VARIATIONS
∽ Can be made easily in smaller units to pack into lunches or to use in picnics as a finger food.
∽ A bit of ground ginger will add flavor. Add ¼ teaspoon with baking soda.

Sliced Lemon Pie

BAKING TIME: *45–55 minutes*
OVEN TEMPERATURE: *400 degrees*

>   *5 large lemons*
>   *2 cups sugar*
>   *1 teaspoon salt*
>   *6 eggs, beaten*

Skin and remove all white from lemons.
Slice thin, remove any seeds, and mix
with sugar and salt. Let stand for at least
2 hours. Add beaten eggs to lemons and
mix very well. Pour into prepared 8-inch
pie crust. Cover with top crust and bake
in a hot oven for 45–55 minutes. Cool on
wire rack. Texture will be considerably
coarser than a modern lemon pie. This
is normal.

Cool in refrigerator and serve in
small slices.

VARIATIONS

∼ Delete top crust and make a meringue
topping. Use 4 egg whites. Add ¼ teaspoon
cream of tartar, ½ cup powdered sugar,
and beat until peaks form. Spoon on carefully and bake for 10 minutes or until nicely
browned.

This goody was a direct result
of simplification of a popular
lemon pie recipe. It was easier to fix
and unusual enough to grab the
attention of any tired ranch hand.
As best can be determined, it was
an adaptation of an old Shaker
recipe developed in Ohio. Old West
bakers sought simplified assembly
while maintaining the core of long
treasured treats. Sliced Lemon Pie
did just that.

Although amazing tales tell
of pioneers assembling pies on
wagon seats, Sliced Lemon Pie
was most likely made on ranches
or settlements, for even this easy
version is a bit awkward for mixing
on the move.

Sliced Lemon Pie is a very
tart dessert, so serving a slice with
whipped cream or a meringue topping
(see Variations) would be ideal.

Sliced Sweet Potato Pie

BAKING TIME: *55 minutes*
OVEN TEMPERATURE: *375 degrees*

> *3 medium sweet potatoes*
>   *(about 1 ½ lbs.)*
> *1 cup brown sugar*
> *¼ teaspoon salt*
> *½ teaspoon nutmeg*
> *1 teaspoon cinnamon*
> *1 egg, beaten*
> *1 tablespoon cornstarch*
> *1 cup cream*
> *¼ cup butter (4 tablespoons)*
> *½ cup chopped pecans*

D espite their endearing flavor and undying popularity, sweet potatoes were nicknamed "music roots" by cowboys. They insisted the root had a pronounced gaseous effect. Although this didn't slow their use, sweet potatoes become the source of many jokes, most of which are better left untold.

The sweet potato pie made in the Old West had little resemblance to today's wonders. Many spices were either not available or too expensive. Original sweet potato pies contained only potato, sugar, lard, eggs, and baking powder. Anything else was a luxury. In defense of this simplicity, the results were surprisingly good.

This recipe comes from an old family album and is unusual because it is spicier than most nineteenth-century varieties. If desired, it can be a double-crusted pie with lattice strips across the top.

Sweet potatoes are normally cooked about 20 minutes in boiling water. However, this recipe requires them to be slightly under-cooked. Peel and boil for only 15 minutes, then cool. Slice (about ¼ inch) and set aside. In a separate bowl, mix brown sugar, salt, nutmeg, and cinnamon. In yet another bowl, mix the beaten egg and cornstarch. Blend with cream. Layer in a 9-inch deep-dish pie crust. Place a layer of sliced sweet potato, sprinkle with sugar and spices, and dot with small pieces of butter. Sprinkle each layer of sweet potatoes with chopped pecans dipped in melted butter. Continue to layer, sprinkle and dot until the pie crust is filled. Carefully pour egg and cream mixture over the

(continued on following page)

masterpiece, and if double crusted, cover with a lattice crust.

Bake in a preheated oven until crust is brown, about 55 minutes.

Best served cool. The pie will set up in about 3–4 hours in a refrigerator. It should be consumed within a few days.

VARIATIONS

∽ For a different taste, add 1 teaspoon grated orange peel to dry ingredients.

∽ For a sweeter pie, reduce brown sugar to ¼ cup and pour ¼ cup honey over layers. Warning, this will be *much* sweeter.

OTHER WILD PLANTS

The new pioneers were surprised at finding so many edible plants about the West. Wild onions were extremely prolific, as were shallots. Shallots—a bit different because encased in a woody,

fibrous covering—produced a very sweet and tasty onion when stripped.

Artichokes, somewhat of a mystery, were identified by one group of travelers as a strange plant tasting exactly like celery. Squash was also abundant. It was not unusual to find pumpkins weighing in at over fifty pounds. Melons, cucumbers, and tomatoes "grew without any attention."

Of course, corn grew throughout the West and was harvested vigorously by Native Americans.

Old West Vinegar Pie

BAKING TIME: *15–20 minutes*
OVEN TEMPERATURE: *350 degrees*

> ⅜ cup granulated sugar
> 3 tablespoons all-purpose flour
> ¼ teaspoon salt
> 1¼ cups hot water
> 3 egg yolks, beaten
> 1 teaspoon lemon extract
> 2 tablespoons butter or margarine
> 2 tablespoons cider vinegar

*V*inegar pie sounds pretty dismal, but it is very similar in taste to lemon pie. It was an extremely popular treat in the Old West, made by chuck wagon and range cooks alike. It was especially appreciated by Westerners who had spent the day on horseback or farming in the dust.

For truly authentic taste, you can make the vinegar as they did at a popular Old West provision store, "[T]ake one large barrel of rain water, carefully add acetic acid, and color to a pleasant tone with burned sugar." Yummy.

Easy to assemble, Vinegar Pie was usually baked in a large Dutch oven immersed in hot embers. Here's the modern way.

Mix sugar, flour, and salt in top of double boiler. Add hot water and mix well. Add beaten egg yolks, lemon extract, butter, and vinegar. Stir, stir, and stir some more. Cook until thickened, about 10–15 minutes. Pour into prepared and prebaked 8-inch pie crust to bake in a preheated oven an additional 15–20 minutes.

Serve chilled.

VARIATIONS
↝ Top with walnuts or pecans mixed with melted butter before baking.
↝ Use egg whites for a meringue topping. Add ¼ teaspoon cream of tartar to beaten egg whites. Whip until stiff. Slowly add 1 tablespoon powdered sugar while beating. Continue to beat until stiff (don't over-beat). Top the pie after it is baked and brown in the same oven about 10 minutes.

Pumpkin Molasses Pie

BAKING TIME: *45–55 minutes*
OVEN TEMPERATURE: *350 degrees*

> 2 cups cooked or canned pumpkin
> 1 cup sour cream
> 1 tablespoon butter, melted
> 3 eggs, beaten
> ½ cup molasses
> ¼ teaspoon salt
> ½ teaspoon ginger
> ½ teaspoon allspice
> 1 teaspoon cinnamon
> ½ teaspoon cloves, ground

For fresh pumpkin, cut a 3–4 pound pumpkin in half. Remove seeds and fibers. Place pumpkin halves face down on a cookie sheet and bake at 375 degrees for 30 minutes or until pumpkin is tender. Scoop out pulp and press to remove excess moisture. Assemble pie filling by mixing all ingredients together in a large bowl, and mix thoroughly. Pour into 9-inch pie crust. Bake in preheated oven. Remove when center has just started to puff. If it has already expanded, the pie is overcooked.

VARIATIONS
⌁ Sprinkle ¼ cup walnuts or pecans over top before placing in oven.
⌁ 2 tablespoons of bourbon added to the pumpkin mix gives the pie a bit of zest.

Transiting pioneers were surprised at finding so many edible plants in the West. Although many were difficult to identify, this didn't stop a frequent trial-and-error approach to recipe development. Many of the subsequent mixes were less than memorable.

Fortunately, squash was easy to recognize and very prolific. Pumpkin, so popular on the East Coast, was easily found in the fall, and if it were not in season, dried pumpkin was available from merchants en route to the new frontier.

The popular pioneer sweetener, molasses, and the use of sour cream give this pie a novel and delicious flavor compared to today's light variety.

Wild Grape–Apple Pie

tremendous variety of apples were available in the Old West. Seedlings were brought out by early settlers, and the trees flourished in the dry heat.

Less well known was the abundance of numerous varieties of grapes growing wild from Oregon to Texas. Both Native Americans and Old West settlers used wild grapes for everything from wine to medicine. The wild western grape was sometimes called the "canyon grape" in recognition of where it seemed to flourish.

Grapes and apples were used in many recipes, but never has a marriage of these fruits been grander than in this luscious pie.

BAKING TIME: *45–55 minutes*
OVEN TEMPERATURE: *400 degrees*

> *2 cups seedless green grapes*
> *4 large peeled and sliced tart apples*
> *1 cup granulated sugar*
> *⅛ teaspoon salt*
> *1 tablespoon orange rind*
> *⅛ teaspoon cinnamon*
> *2 tablespoons cornstarch*
> *3 tablespoons butter, cubed*

In one bowl, mix grapes, apples (sliced thinly), sugar, salt, orange rind, and cinnamon, and cornstarch. Let sit for 10–15 minutes while the sugar pulls out juice from the apples. Pour entire mix into a prepared 9-inch pie shell and dapple with butter pieces. Cover with a pastry crust and bake for 45–55 minutes.

Yes, ice cream works wonders with a slice of this. Serve pie warm or cold. Keeps for about 4 days in the refrigerator.

VARIATIONS
↪ To accelerate baking, cook the mixed ingredients in a saucepan over medium heat for 10–15 minutes; then pour into prepared shell. This should reduce the baking time to 30 minutes.

(continued on following page)

↩ Use ½ teaspoon nutmeg in addition to, or in place of, cinnamon.
↩ For a real creative flare, add ½ cup blueberries and reduce grapes by ½ cup.

APPLE FACTS

Old West residents had many functions for apples besides eating. A wedge placed in a cookie tin helped keep cookies soft in dry climates. Also, though pioneers may have not understood why, apples also helped ripen other fruits. When apples were

stationed nearby, the ethylene gas they gave off accelerated the ripening process of pears and other fruits normally slow to ripen. Another celebrated Old West apple product was cider. Apple cider was inexpensive, long-keeping, and delicious. But, to the dismay of the temperance movement and delight of many cowpokes, cider also fermented exceptionally well. Fermenting hard cider could easily generate an alcohol content of five percent or more. It was rumored that entire apple orchards were cut down by some temperance organizations to prevent the manufacture of hard cider. It must have been incredible stuff. Hard apple cider isn't on the neighborhood shelves anymore, but if you're so inclined, there are dozens of books for do-it-yourselfers on how to go about fermenting the real thing.

On the other hand, applesauce was accepted as a pure alternative. The popular mash was simple to make over a campfire just by cooking apples down to mush, then adding a bit of sweetener and spices. Served hot or cold, it was a genuine treat after a dusty day on the trail.

YEP, WE'RE OUTTA COFFEE

On the horrendously difficult cattle drives, there was nothing like a hot cup of coffee to warm a chilly evening. If coffee was too expensive, or a shipment failed to arrive at the General Store, the trail boss would ask the chuck wagon cook to counterfeit beans. Various plants and nuts were baked, browned, and mixed with what little coffee was left in an attempt to resemble the familiar java. This would hold off the hired hands for about a week, after which the help either abandoned the boss or rode miles away to borrow the precious bean from another rancher.

Although no cowboy worth his hat would try anything but coffee on the range, Native Americans knew better. They had an expanded beverage line that included local foliage. For example, teas were extremely popular warm drinks among a variety of tribes. They were prevalent as both a simple beverage and as an integral part in tribal ceremonies. Teas were easy to make and blend. Leaves, roots, or an assembly of various dried succulents were used for the beverage. The most popular were cota and lip fern. Native Americans tried other blends such as boiled Gambel Oak bark, ground Chechil acorns, and strained walnuts in warm drinks. Although little is written about these original drinks, they were popular for centuries.

At the other end of the spectrum was "Tiʒwin." It was an alcoholic beverage only those raised with the mixture could appreciate. Mescal plant hearts were cooked until they were gluey. A mash was strained to extract a liquid they allowed to ferment. Its potency was legendary.

Pioneer Pie Crust

T'S AS EASY AS PIE." WHOEVER SAID THIS PROBABLY DIDN'T MAKE many pie crusts. Fillings are indeed simple affairs; the downfall is a soggy or tough crust. Probably no other part of the pie is as scrutinized as the crust. A delicious crust enhances an excellent pie. A tough crust discourages the same compliments.

Most pie crusts of the nineteenth century were made with flour of questionable quality, but consumers still described them as delectable. Some of these comments can be dismissed as those made by pie eaters who would eat raw cactus if it were sweet enough, but certainly others knew exactly what they were eating.

Little was documented on crust preparation techniques. Instead the procedure was passed on by talented bakers to the next generation. Virtually every woman of the era knew what made up a wonderful crust. Assembly was not by trial and error or through picture book instructions that many must cope with today.

Consistent quality crusts can be assembled in every kitchen following a few rules:

- All ingredients should be cool. Unfortunately, pioneers did not have any method of chilling ingredients, but the winter months made much better crusts.
- Work quickly and lightly. Never overwork the pastry.
- Roll out on a cold platform, such as marble. Pioneers used to roll dough out on wagon seats, so dough can take some abuse. Flattening between two sheets of waxed paper works nicely too.
- Roll out at least 1 inch larger than the pie plate to allow for shrinkage and trimming.
- Do not grease the pie pan. Just place the crust inside the well, and don't stretch it or it will shrink in the oven.

Short Pastry

A more crumbly texture than flaky, Short Pastry was extremely popular for fruit tarts.

2½ cups flour
½ teaspoon salt
½ cup solid shortening
¼ cup butter or margarine
4 tablespoons ice water

Blend flour and salt. Chill shortening and butter. Add to flour by cutting in with two knives or a pastry knife. Keep cutting and slowly add ice water. Chill thoroughly before rolling out to ¼ inch thick.

Bread Crumb Crust

When short of flour or long in stale bread, this was a good option. Here, butter is substituted for lard, and sugar is added to bring to modern tastes.

2 cups dry, fine bread crumbs
½ cup soft butter or margarine
½ teaspoon salt
2 tablespoons powdered sugar

There is no gluten to destroy by over-working this recipe, so add all ingredients together in a bowl and mix with hands. Squeeze and stir until blended, and pat into ungreased pie pan. Prebake at 425 degrees for 8–10 minutes for cream pies.

Venerable Puddings

*Morgan and Trimble's Cow Camp, Dolores Plateau,
Dolores County, Colorado, July 1902.*

Puddings: From Main Dish to Dessert

N O AMERICAN COOKBOOK OF THE NINETEENTH CENTURY WORTH its paper would have been complete without pudding recipes. Puddings were the dessert of choice for many living in and traveling to the Old West.

Puddings were originally developed as a main dish. Fourteenth-century English "puddynges" were boiled in sausage casing and served as an entree, even at the most lavish buffets. Ingredients included just about anything the designated chef found exciting. Later, special cloths or bags were used to hold the mix. They simplified preparation, but they also seemed to foreshadow the demise of puddings as a centerpiece for dinner.

Pudding as a dessert is a relatively contemporary form of this five-hundred-year-old dish. Because of an increase in the use of sweeteners about two centuries ago, innovative cooks transformed puddings into a post-dinner treat. The pudding base was a perfect medium to hold sweeter flavors just coming into use.

Puddings differ slightly from their close cousins, custards. In puddings, eggs are rarely separated, and the preparation techniques are not quite as critical. Unlike custards, puddings generally do not require precooking before assembly and will not rise as dramatically. The use of puddings for rough-riding occupants of the Old West made much more sense.

Puddings Move West

When pudding recipes traveled with explorers to America, the new inhabitants were surprised to discover they weren't the only ones with good puddings. Native Americans introduced European settlers to a number of exciting foods.

Pictured from top are Spotted Pup (page 143) and Sugar-Spice Pudding (page 144).

One of the most popular dishes was a corn-based pudding, later called "Indian Pudding" in eighteenth-century cookbooks.

With the shortage of wheat, the colonists found this variant every bit as good, and far more practical, than their own. Puddings continued to develop in Colonial kitchens with cooks merging the best of the two cultures. Incorporation of fruits and other ingredients indigenous to their new surroundings resulted in pudding's ranking as the most popular dessert of the day. So, it's understandable why puddings went west on wagon trains. Virtually every cook and baker of the Old West had a favorite mix. Recipes cataloged in personal journals abound, some more palatable than others.

It's not clear why puddings have lost such popularity. Whereas older cookbooks offered one hundred or more pudding recipes, modern recipe books of the last forty years offer few. Of course, packaged puddings are present in quick-open snack packs in most food markets. However, as broad as modern cuisines are, puddings share little space on many contemporary menus. Granted, old recipes calling for boiling a dessert mash in an intestine won't tweak modern culinary senses, but doing the same in a pudding tin or reasonable facsimile would make a marvelous presentation. Various shapes, sizes, and toppings (found at the end of the chapter) are possible to satisfy even the fussiest eater.

Preparation

Puddings can be boiled, baked, or steamed. Boiling is accomplished by total immersion of special cloths or bags, but steaming and baking are much simpler.

Steaming

Steaming puddings was a popular Old West preparation method and still remains a good technique today. Unfortunately, the richness and flavors of each mix vary widely, so it's difficult to make many universal rules. Some recipes listed in this chapter may include an exception to the general practice, so be cautious and carefully read the instructions for each.

The good news is that puddings are seldom wrapped in cloths or sausage casings for boiling or steaming anymore. Pudding tins took their place and allowed cooks to steam the mix, a much faster and cleaner solution. If a pudding tin is not in your kitchen inventory, fret not; almost anything can be used. If it can stand steaming, it can be a designated pudding tin. Even small bowls, well greased and topped with some kind of lid, are excellent steaming containers. Of course, a mold of some kind will greatly enhance the pudding presentation. Just make sure it fits into the steaming pot of choice.

The pudding container sits in a bed of water for steaming. The circulating steam cooks the mix rapidly and evenly, so it is important to keep the water boiling. Dry heat will quickly ruin your creation. Our pudding recipes call for steaming times from ten minutes to one hour, mostly because of size rather than type of ingredients. The pot bears watching. It's not difficult, just a matter of being mindful.

Here, then, are some guidelines for steaming:

- Fill pudding tins only two-thirds full to allow for expansion.
- Elevate molds in the steamer. Use a trivet or anything else to lift the pudding mold at least a half-inch above the bottom of the kettle.
- Tightly cover the pudding mold. Oiled cloth works nicely and will allow for pudding expansion.
- Cook just below the boiling point of water. This ensures even heat and slower evaporation of water.
- After steaming, remove cover and cool down immediately in a bed of cold water. If you don't do this, the pudding will continue to cook.

Baking

For some, baking represents a far simpler method of pudding preparation. In reality, it is not that far removed from steaming because a moist oven is necessary for the pudding to set properly.

Whereas steamed pudding is contained in a small pot of boiling water, baked pudding sits in a bath of water that provides the steam.

Most of the rules for baking are the same as steaming:

- Fill the mold only two-thirds full to allow for expansion.
- Tightly cover the pudding mold, preferably with oiled cloth. This allows for pudding expansion, and the pudding can breathe.
- Set the mold in a bath of water. This can be anything from a roasting pan to an oven-proof pot.

∽ The water should be steaming, not boiling. The recommended temperatures in the chapter's recipes can be adjusted accordingly.

Unmolding Your Treasure

To unmold the pudding, run a very sharp knife around the inside of the mold. Place a serving plate on top, and turn the whole thing over. The pudding should slide out easily. If not, place a warm towel over the mold and tap lightly.

Apple-Rice Pudding

BAKING TIME: *30 minutes*
OVEN TEMPERATURE: *300 degrees*

1 cup cooked rice
2 cups milk
2 eggs, separated
½ cup granulated sugar
¼ teaspoon salt
4 tablespoons butter, melted
3 large apples, cored, skinned, diced
1 teaspoon vanilla
1 teaspoon cinnamon

Heat rice and milk in a saucepan. In two separate bowls, beat egg whites until stiff and yolks until lemon-colored. Add sugar and salt to beaten egg yolks. Add ½ cup of hot mixture to egg yolk mix. Stir, then add all of egg mix to saucepan. Cook until thickened, about 10–15 minutes. Add all remaining ingredients except egg whites and stir. Fold in egg whites and place in buttered dish. Bake in preheated oven in a bed of water for about 30 minutes, until firm.

VARIATIONS
↪ Other fruits work fine—prunes, peaches, apricots and the like. Be sure to drain well.
↪ For extra zip, use brown sugar instead of granulated sugar. Break up any chunks before mixing.

*B*oth apples and rice were relatively plentiful in the latter years of the migration west. The cooks carried dried and reconstituted fruits to serve plain or mixed with various dishes.

Unfortunately, rice had a more difficult time being accepted, largely because of the cooks' preparation guesswork. Disasters were monumental. Once ingredient measurements were figured out, rice became a real treat on the range. Bakers found highly creative uses for it such as rice muffins and spotted pup.

This recipe could have been made by many frontier cooks.

Bread Pudding

BAKING TIME: *50 minutes*
OVEN TEMPERATURE: *350 degrees*

½ cup granulated sugar
3–4 cups milk
3 cups stale bread, cubed
3 eggs, beaten
½ teaspoon nutmeg
1 tablespoon butter, melted
1 teaspoon vanilla

Dissolve sugar into 3 cups milk. Soak bread cubes for a half-hour in milk to moisten thoroughly. Mix eggs, nutmeg, melted butter, and vanilla. Pour all into a large 9-inch bread pan or baking dish. Sprinkle top with extra granulated sugar and nutmeg. Bake about 1 hour in a pan of water.

Chill bread pudding and serve seated in a bed of warm cream.

VARIATIONS
⌒ Raisins, prunes, or apples are a natural for bread pudding. Add ½ cup with soaking bread.

*L*ittle could be wasted on the frontier. Uses were found for everything edible, and bread was no exception. If it couldn't be brought back from rock-hard staleness, it was used for bread crumbs, added to beans, or made into ever-popular bread pudding.

Pudding recipes and techniques were brought to the open range by European descendants who remembered them as a rich and easy dessert. With the limited selection of ingredients found in the Old West, a bread base was a natural choice. It turned out to be the best choice anyway. Bread held moisture well, and it resulted in a very tender and nicely textured pudding.

Original mixtures were made with bread and water. For richness, we'll substitute luxurious milk.

Baked Indian Pudding

BAKING TIME: *1½ hours*
OVEN TEMPERATURE: *300 degrees*

> *3 cups whole milk*
> *½ cup cornmeal*
> *½ cup molasses*
> *¼ cup butter or margarine*
> *1 egg, beaten*
> *¼ cup sugar*
> *¼ teaspoon salt*
> *dash cinnamon & ginger*

In a sauce pan, mix milk and molasses. Stir in cornmeal. Cook over medium heat and stir until thickened (about 10 minutes). Remove from heat and add butter. In a separate bowl, mix egg, sugar, salt, and spices to taste. Add ½ cup of hot mixture to egg-sugar mix. Stir. Then add egg-sugar mix to hot mix. Stir again. Pour into a one-quart casserole dish seated in bed of water. Bake in medium oven. Top will spring to the touch when done.

Best served with Lemon Sauce (page 148).

There are no reliable references on where this originated. My suspicion is that it's very much like Indian frybread, invented by pioneers and borrowed by Native Americans. (See Frybread, page 158.) Most everything of the era was labeled "Indian" if it had a trace of corn.

Baked Indian Pudding appears in recipe books as far back as 1856. Because the original mix was easy to blend and short on ingredients, it had all the makings of a very popular range food. As newer recipes evolved, more variety appeared in Indian pudding's list of ingredients, satisfying modern tastes. This recipe falls somewhere in the middle of Indian pudding lineage.

All listed components were available to pioneers by 1860, but many were cost prohibitive. As the country's distribution system matured, prices of goods fell to levels where all could enjoy a wider selection of options.

Molasses Pudding

STEAMING TIME: *2 hours*

> *2 cups cold water*
> *1 cup molasses*
> *2 eggs, beaten*
> *½ cup butter or margarine, melted*
> *1 cup flour*
> *1 teaspoon baking soda*
> *1 cup raisins*

Thoroughly grease pudding mold. Mix water, molasses, eggs, and butter. Heat in a saucepan until butter is melted. In a separate bowl, blend flour and baking soda. Add to water-molasses mix and blend well until smooth; a whisk works nicely. Pour all into mold and stir in raisins. Set mold into a bed of water. Cover pot and steam for about 2 hours.

*N*o pudding selection would be complete without a molasses dish. It was the sweetener of choice, because it was often the only sweetener within miles.

The bottom of the barrel when processing sugar was sorghum. It was inexpensive and plentiful because few living in civilized centers back East would ever consider using such a "vile" product. This attitude was certainly understandable because it wasn't very sweet, and many dishes were overwhelmed with sorghum to give them a sugary flavor. The next grade up was blackstrap, and it wasn't much better. It still required a heavy hand if a dish were to taste sweet, but the price was right. For those who could afford it, light molasses offered a delicate flavor and sumptuous sweetness. It's what we use here, so eat like an affluent cowpoke.

If you would really rather stick to the original flavoring, sorghum and blackstrap are still available through bakery supply houses.

Pictured opposite, clockwise from upper left, are Bread Pudding (page 134), Molasses Pudding (this page), and Baked Indian Pudding (page 135).

OLD WEST COOKING DICTIONARY

AIRTIGHTS: *All canned goods.*

BEAR SIGN: *Similar to the modern donut.*

CALF FRIES: *Branding time.*

CANNED COWBOY: *Canned milk; real milk was hard to get.*

CHARLIE TAYLOR: *A butter substitute of sorghum and bacon grease.*

CHIP WAGON: *A wagon dedicated to carrying campfire "prairie coal."*

CHUCK: *Range cowboy's word for any food.*

CHUCK WAGON CHICKEN: *Bacon, also called "Kansas City fish."*

COONEY: *Hammock streched under a chuck wagon, also "possum belly."*

COW GREASE: *Real butter.*

DOUGH KEG: *The wooden barrel containing the sourdough starter.*

EATIN' IRONS: *Utensils: fork, spoon and knife.*

FEED BAG: *Ranch eating place; also "mess house" or "nose bag."*

FIRKIN: *The sourdough container on a chuck wagon, also "dough keg."*

GREASY SACK OUTFIT: *Not using a chuck wagon but packouts on mules.*

GRUBPILE: *A call from the cook to "come 'n' get it."*

GUT ROBBER: *The cook, also "bean master" or "biscuit roller."*

HOG SIDE: *Salt pork used in cooking and some baking, also "Old Ned."*

LICK: *Molasses, also called "blackstrap" or "larrup."*

MOUNTAIN OYSTERS: *Calf testes roasted as a between-meal snack.*

MUSIC ROOTS: *Sweet potatoes with a pronounced gaseous effect.*

OVERLAND TROUT: *Pigs and hogs, sometimes bacon.*

POSSUM BELLY: *A hammock stretched below the chuck wagon for cargo.*

PRAIRIE COAL: *Cow or buffalo manure, dried and used in campfires.*

PRAIRIE STRAWBERRIES: *Red beans, also called "Arizona Strawberries."*

SEA PLUMS: *Oysters (canned).*

SKUNK EGG: *An onion.*

SOFT GRUB: *Hotel or diner food.*

SQUIRREL CAN: *Large can used for after-meal scraps.*

SUCKEYES: *Pancakes.*

SWAMP SEED: *Rice.*

TEXAS BUTTER: *A butter substitute of hot lard, flour, and water.*

WOOL ON A HANDLE: *A lamb chop, generally despised by cattlemen.*

WRECK PANS: *Pans filled with water to accept dirty dishes.*

Oatmeal Pudding

BAKING TIME: *50–60 minutes*
OVEN TEMPERATURE: *325 degrees*

2 cups boiling milk
1 cup rolled oats
½ cup sugar
½ cup dry bread crumbs
2 tablespoons butter, melted
2 eggs, beaten
½ teaspoon lemon extract
½ cup chopped dried fruit

Pour boiling milk into rolled oats and sugar. Stir. When mix is cooled and sugar dissolved, add bread crumbs. Mix should be stiff but able to be stirred. Add more milk if too stiff or more oatmeal if not stiff enough. Then add melted butter, eggs, and lemon. Fold in dried fruit. Use raisins, apricots, apples, or peaches. Bake in a well-buttered, covered dish for 50–60 minutes. Best if placed in a bed of water in the oven, but it is not necessary.

Serve when cool, covered in Lemon Sauce (page 148).

There probably wasn't a child of the Old West who hadn't tried oatmeal. Despite this popularity, though, some older sources say oats were originally grown for animal feed and best kept that way. Undoubtedly, they say this because whole oats must be hulled before they're fit for human consumption, a considerable effort for many decades. However, when hulled, the oat product was referred to as groats, and these were available at any number of Old West supply stores.

Many mills offered to process oats further, both before and after the sale. When steamed and crushed between steel rollers, they became rolled oats, perfect for cereals and fillers for other foods. Because of the shortage of many other baking supplies, rolled oats appeared in cakes, breads, and puddings. This pudding recipe is a classic use of oats.

The only fundamental change to the original recipe is a thoughtful substitution of butter for shredded suet.

Prune Pudding

Although not often discussed in Old West journals, records from old supply houses indicated prunes were used throughout the area. Prunes were simply dried plums, but it had to be a plum high enough in natural sugar to prevent exterior or interior decay while drying. Most were grown and dried in the East and shipped to suppliers in the Midwest for distribution in the West. Distribution usually entailed marketing to the wagon trains starting west from Kansas or Missouri. Later in the nineteenth century, the railroad carried tons of prunes to new residents anxious for sweet fruits.

Prunes had many benefits. Pound for pound they were high in nutrients and low in cost, and they kept well. They were close to a perfect food for folk burning countless calories a day.

BAKING TIME: *30 minutes*
OVEN TEMPERATURE: *325 degrees*

1 pound prunes
½ cup sugar
2 cups milk
4 eggs, beaten
½ teaspoon vanilla
1 cup flour

Wash prunes and place into a pot. Cover with cold water and soak for 2 hours. Cook prunes over medium heat in the same pot until soft, about 10–15 minutes. Let cool. Drain, remove prune pits, and cut into small pieces. Place prune pieces into a bowl and stir in sugar. Mix in milk, eggs, and vanilla. Slowly add flour and mix until well blended. Butter a small baking dish; pour in prunes and milk mix. Bake covered and immersed in a pan of water for 25–30 minutes or until firm.

Serve with a sweet custard sauce or whipped cream.

Hasty Pudding

COOKING TIME: *15–20 minutes*
STOVE TEMPERATURE: *medium*

> *1 cup cornmeal*
> *1 cup cold water*
> *3 cups boiling water*
> *½ teaspoon salt*

In a bowl, combine cornmeal, and water. Add ½ teaspoon salt to 2 cups boiling water. Slowly add cornmeal to boiling water and cook over low heat, stirring occasionally. Will cook completely in about 10–15 minutes.

Serve with butter, molasses, maple syrup, brown sugar, or anything else sweet.

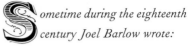

Sometime during the eighteenth century Joel Barlow wrote:

I sing the sweets I know,
the charms I feel,
My morning incense,
and my evening meal,
The sweets of Hasty Pudding.

Hasty Puddings generally refer to a variety of puddings that were very popular with Old West cooks because of easy preparation. As far as many cooks were concerned, if a dish were palatable and reasonably simple to prepare, it was served. However, this doesn't necessarily mean it was well liked by all consumers.

Referred to as "mush" by more than one cowpoke on a cattle drive, Hasty Pudding probably wore out its welcome after the first month. Only so much can be mixed into the batter. Some bitterly complained that Hasty Puddings did little to live up to their name. Cookbooks and journals say that the secret of good "mush" is to ensure it is boiled for at least an hour.

Hardly quick, this is faster than some other alternatives. The flavoring is very basic.

Apple Corn Bread Charlotte

BAKING TIME: *none*

Base:
    1 Apple-Corn Loaf (see page 10)
Filling:
    ¼ *ounce gelatin*
    ¼ *cup cold water*
    1 tablespoon vanilla
    1 pint whipping cream
    4 tablespoons powdered sugar

Charlottes were created by the inventer of classic French cooking, Marie-Antoine Careme, for the arrival of Louis XVIII and his royal family. When Careme was sent across the channel in the late eighteenth century to cook for the English, the wondrous Charlotte Russe went with him. Charlottes quickly made their way to the new world and were appropriately modified for emerging Colonial tastes.

Americans settling in the West called it "icebox cake," and it was made for special occasions at finer western ranch houses. This Charlotte required no cooking but did need cooling for at least four hours, fairly easy in the crisp desert evenings.

This recipe, with ingredients common to the Old West, was developed from a recipe found in an 1890 California cookbook.

Cut apple corn loaf in about ¼-inch-thick slices. Line the bottom of a spring form pan with waxed paper. Lay slices of loaf on the bottom of pan. Do not leave gaps. Cut oblong slices and line the sides of the pan. Place very close together so there are no gaps. Brush with cream or apple cider to seal.

Let gelatin stand in water for 5 minutes; then dissolve over low heat. Add vanilla. While cooling, whip cream and add powdered sugar. Beat until stiff. When gelatin is cool, quickly stir it into the cream. Pour mix into prepared pan. Cool in refrigerator 4–5 hours before serving.

Turn out on a large serving platter. Remove springform pan and slice like cake. To update, sprinkle with apple liqueur and top with a sauce.

Spotted Pup

BAKING TIME: *1 hour*
OVEN TEMPERATURE: *325 degrees*

2 cups prepared rice
1⅓ cups whole milk
½ cup brown sugar
1 tablespoon soft butter or margarine
1 teaspoon vanilla
2 eggs, beaten
½ cup raisins

Prepare rice and set aside to cool. In a separate bowl, combine remaining ingredients (except raisins) and mix. Now stir in the rice and raisins until well blended. Grease a baking dish and pour in the mix. Cover and place in a pan of hot water; bake for 60 minutes.

Serve hot or cold in a small dish. Top with a dash of cinnamon or nutmeg.

VARIATION
∼ The pudding can also be baked in a prepared pie shell or a bed of cookie crumbs. Be sure to use a well-greased pan.

By far one of the Old West's most popular desserts, Spotted Pup was made on the range by chuck wagon cooks and farmhouse gourmets alike.

Where the name evolved is anyone's guess, but it certainly is appropriate. Spotted Pup was a white rice pudding mixed with a healthy quantity of raisins, taking on the appearance of a Dalmatian to most eyes. Without the raisins, it was not only disdained, but called just "pup."

This modern version is a bit more palatable, even without the normal addition of creek water.

Sugar-Spice Pudding

ugar is so accessible today, it's difficult to imagine it as a luxury. One hundred fifty years ago, tons of "sugar loaves" were imported from Cuba and sold throughout the country. It proved to be a very lucrative market, but was relatively expensive to purchase and difficult to find in large amounts in the Old West.

Sugar was eventually sold in blocks or "loaves." It was easy to package and transport. Sugar augers or specially designed sugar nippers were necessary to break apart the hard cube. Then the chunks were pounded fine. Sometimes placing the pieces through a coffee grinder proved faster. Finally (for those concerned about sanitation), impurities were removed by sifting or washing.

Thus, not only was sugar cost prohibitive, but it was also considerable work just to get ready. If it was found on chuck wagons or pioneers' wagons, it was undoubtedly already processed and loosely packaged.

Here, then, is an honest-to-goodness treat for those out west.

BAKING TIME: *2 hours*
OVEN TEMPERATURE: *300 degrees*

½ cup sugar
2 tablespoons flour
2 eggs, separated
2 cups milk
2 tablespoons butter or margarine
1 teaspoon vanilla
⅛ teaspoon allspice
⅛ teaspoon nutmeg
½ teaspoon cinnamon
¼ teaspoon cream of tartar

Mix sugar and flour. In a separate bowl, mix beaten egg yolks and milk. Slowly add milk mixture to sugar and flour, stirring all the while. Bring to boil stirring constantly. Add butter, vanilla, and spices. Remove from heat. Whip egg whites with cream of tartar until peaks form and fold carefully into custard. Pour custard into a well-buttered dish and place dish in a pan of hot water. Bake until set, about 2 hours.

Chill and serve with Lemon Sauce or Vanilla Sauce (page 148).

Son-of-a-Bitch-in-a-Sack

STEAMING TIME: *2 hours*

1 cup flour
1 teaspoon baking powder
½ teaspoon salt
1 cup granulated sugar
¼ cup soft butter or margarine
½ teaspoon vanilla
2 eggs, beaten
1 cup whole milk
½ cup raisins

Sift flour, baking powder, and salt together, and set aside. Cream the sugar, butter, and vanilla together until light. Add eggs and beat in. This can be done by hand (spoon or whisk) or food processor (much easier). Alternately add sifted ingredients and milk.

Grease a covered pudding mold and fill two-thirds full with mix. Drop in raisins and cover. Place on top a trivet in a large kettle, with an inch of water, to steam for 2 hours. Note: the water will need to be replenished at least three times, so watch closely.

After cooling and setting up, unmold and place on a nice serving dish.

VARIATION
⤳ Chop 1 cup fresh suet very fine and add to raisins. Also add a shot of brandy with the milk.

This extremely popular concoction was made by mixing flour, sugar, salt, baking powder, and local creek water into a soft mass. For flavor, soaked raisins and suet were then added. The entire mixture was put into a sack, hung in a large hot water bucket, then placed on a pot rack over coals to steam. The results were highly variable depending on the cook's skill. If not steamed just right, it would become a loosely jellied mass, whose closest cousin could be called a sauce. The name must have come from a cowpoke's disappointment in the result of one evening's attempt at the unique dessert.

To duplicate this for a modern party treat, a few items are added to stabilize the process and make it a bit more predictable. Suet was deleted, but feel free to add a cup. If you have the fortitude to add suet, see Variations for mixing instructions.

GET YOUR CAN IN HERE

What we now take for granted has a very spotty past. In the early 1800s, the English invented a new process of storing meats and vegetables in airtight, tinned iron containers. It came to America by 1850 as "tin cans" to service a mobile population.

Manufacturing was rather simple. Food stuff was jammed into the can, covered and boiled with only a little vent remaining open for expanding air. When most of the hot air was out, the hole was soldered closed by hand. It was thought that the expulsion of air was the purifying process to keep goods fresh, when in reality it was the boiling. As a result of this thinking, more than a few were poisoned by improperly processed canning. By 1870, manufacturers finally applied the lessons of Pasteur's study in purification, and most problems were solved—except taste.

Although the flavor of canned goods had only a distant relationship with the taste of fresh food, in the absence of a local farm, it did give the cook a chance at peas, beans, and so on to expand the bill of fare. In our American Old West, cowboys coined canned foods "airtights." Despite less than ideal flavor, they did provide some relief from sowbelly stew and beans.

Another bonus of having a limited selection of tinned cans about was label recitation. Things would get slow around the campfire and a favorite game was to recall the entire label verbatim. Of course, the appropriate penalities would be levied for any errors.

Even today, some western ranch hands use canned tomatoes as a thirst quencher on dusty rides.

Sauces: Sweet Rewards

"THE PROOF OF THE PUDDING IS IN THE EATING," WROTE Miguel de Cervantes in *Don Quixote de la Mancha*. As fun as pudding preparation may be, eating the lovely result is the true reward. Few desserts are so joyfully enhanced by a variety of toppings. A number of sauce recipes follow. Try them; the sweetness of each can be adjusted to suit the most fickle tastes.

Sauces should be warmed prior to being used as a topping or a base for the pudding. Serving the sauce in a gravy boat will allow guests to sweeten the pudding to their own taste. A spectacular sight, and delicious variant to sweet sauce, is to flambé. Pour warm brandy over the top of the pudding, light with a match, and serve.

No pudding is complete without a sweet, tasty topping. Here are a few of the most popular mentioned in the memoirs of those who lived in the new frontier. Most require light cooking, but are quickly and easily prepared.

SWEET PACKAGES

Sugar was packaged as loaves or cones. Cones were manufactured by pouring hot sugar syrup mixes into molds, with a string running through the middle to hang it for display.

Wrapped in dark blue paper, it was instantly recognizable in any market. In the Old West world of letting nothing go to waste, the blue paper was soaked and the resulting indigo blue water was used as a dye.

Lemon Sauce

½ cup butter
⅜ cup sugar
2 eggs, beaten
2 tablespoons lemon juice
1 teaspoon nutmeg
½ cup hot water

Melt butter and mix with sugar. Beat in egg and lemon juice. Mix in nutmeg and pour hot water over all and blend. Place over double boiler and cook over low heat. When thickened, remove from heat and serve. A tablespoon or two of brandy can be blended in easily before serving, if desired.

Vanilla Sauce

1 tablespoon flour
1 cup water
2 tablespoons granulated sugar
2 tablespoons butter or margarine
1 teaspoon vanilla

Mix flour with a few tablespoons water and mix until pasty. Pour a full cup of water and remaining ingredients into saucepan. Boil and stir constantly. When the mixture has the consistency of gravy, remove from heat and serve.

Butterscotch Sauce

¼ cup water
1 cup brown sugar
3 tablespoons corn syrup
¼ cup butter
1 teaspoon vanilla

Place water, brown sugar, and corn syrup into saucepan and bring to a boil. Sauce should bubble. Boil down about 5 minutes over medium heat. Remove. Stir in butter and vanilla. Serve.

Cinnamon Sauce

½ cup whipping cream
¼ cup butter
1 teaspoon cinnamon
1 tablespoon sugar

Add all to sauce pan. Mix well and boil down until consistency is like gravy. Serve immediately.

CACTUS: A TREAT FOR EVERYONE

Most pioneers traveling through the desert pushed aside cactus as a nuisance plant, but a few of the more creative cooks and bakers quickly learned from area Native Americans how versatile it was. Familiar varieties of agave, prickly pear, saguaro, and yucca were of enormous importance to Native American diet for centuries.

It's easy to understand the popularity of cactus fruit. Most are surprisingly sweet. With a shortage of sugar on the range, cooking or baking with cactus mash worked wonders. The mash or juice was added to quick breads and puddings for a sweet zip unmatched by any other ingredient.

This thorned sugarcane of the West is little used today except for occasional prickly pear candy experienced at the local shops.

Whipped Cream

2 cups whipping cream
¼ cup sugar
⅛ teaspoon vanilla

Add all and stir until sugar is dissolved.
Beat until peaks form in whipping cream.
Serve immediately. It will not keep long.

HOME, HOME ON THE RANGE

Conditions for the first settlers in the Old West were deplorable. Although a few cattle barons lived in walnut-paneled mansions, the masses lived in considerably

more humble surroundings.
Most small ranch homes were covered wagons, tents, or dirt huts. Middle-class homes were one-room huts carved into the sides of hills and roofed with either sod or branches. Dirt served as the floor of choice for most of the homesteader population. Mattresses were feedbags sewn together and filled with "Montana Feathers," better known as hay.
Cooking and baking was done the chuck wagon cook way, around campfires. Utensils were whatever was carried on the trip to new homes. As homesteaders carved out a living, a few luxuries appeared, such as wood structures, to keep out most of the snakes, scorpions, mice, and spiders.

For true comfort, a Franklin Stove was a treasured accessory for baking. The kitchen, or food preparation area, was one of the most important spots in any ranch home and deserved the best one could afford. It's easy to understand why. Eating was one of the few exciting social events in an otherwise difficult existence.

Extra~Special Stuff

Taos woman baking bread, ca. 1900–1920.

"Dough Nuts" and Other Miscellaneous Blends

LD WEST PIONEERS, CHUCK WAGON COOKS, AND RANCH HOUSE
bakers found the shortage of ingredients challenging. If goods
were available, sometimes cost was so prohibitive that it made
purchase impractical. In the early 1800s, published recipe books
were primarily collections from kitchens in the Deep South or
from large East Coast cities. There, fresh fruits and vegetables were always
obtainable, and stoves a bit more sophisticated.

The West had no such fortune until the late nineteenth century, so it's
remarkable anything was made as well as it was. Personal journals logged some
of the more popular Old West dishes, but information was rarely passed on
in the form of published recipes. In what little information was shared, only
vague references were made to products and ingredients. Virtually nothing was
written about preparation. For example, the recipe for "heavenly" Houn' Ears
& Whirlups (page 159) was recorded in numerous cowboy logs, but apparently
never by anyone who had to assemble the dish. One can surmise from described
texture and taste how they were made, but it is still conjecture.

This chapter is dedicated to many of those miscellaneous blends made on the
new frontier. Not all were baked, but they used many of the same ingredients
and were so popular as treats that they simply can't be excluded.

*Pictured, clockwise from top left, are Bear Sign (page 154), Jumbles (page 161), and Splatter
Dabs (page 170).*

Bear Sign

ogged in an obscure nine-
teenth-century autobiography
of a cowboy was talk of a pastry
called "bear sign." That his friends
would make excuses to ride twenty
miles in a hard saddle to a local
cook making the popular pastry was
testimony to its standing. From the
popularity of this item, one would
think it came from the heavens.
What it appears to be is an open-
range version of the ever-popular
donut, western-style.

Bear signs came in as many
varieties as an imagination would
allow. Most were assembled without
the well-known hole, for that was a
European creation. They were also
called "oily cakes" or "dough nuts."

Combining a number of old
western recipes, here's a delicious
fail-safe mix you'll enjoy.

FRYING TIME: *3–5 minutes per side*
FRYING TEMPERATURE: *375 degrees*

1 cup buttermilk
2 eggs, beaten
1 cup granulated sugar
⅛ cup butter or margarine, melted
2 tablepoons baking powder
½ teaspoon salt
½ teaspoon cinnamon
4 cups all-purpose flour

In the first bowl, mix buttermilk, eggs,
sugar, and melted butter until well blended. In a second bowl, combine the baking
powder, salt, cinnamon, and flour. Slowly
add the dry ingredients to the first bowl,
stirring them together. This mix should be
stiff enough to hold a spoon upright; if
not, mix in more flour. Knead together
lightly for a minute or so, then turn out on
a floured board or countertop.

Use a rolling pin, empty bottle, or the
heel of your hand to roll out to about one
finger-width high (¼ inch). Cut circles out
with a small glass and set aside for about
5 minutes.

Meanwhile, pour 1 inch of oil in a
large skillet and heat (cast iron can't be
beat). It's hot enough when a bread cube
browns in about 1 minute. Slide the circles
into the frying pan and brown one side.

(continued on following page)

Turn over and brown on the other. Set out to drain on a plate covered with paper towels.

Cover with powdered sugar and eat warm.

VARIATIONS

↬ When mixing, add 1 teaspoon lemon extract or ½ teaspoon nutmeg for flavor.
↬ Cut the rolled out dough into strips instead of circles.
↬ Pour a hot fruit sauce on top and serve in a bowl.

Yeast-Raised Bear Sign

FRYING TIME: *about 2 minutes*
FRYING TEMPERATURE: *375 degrees*

1 cup whole milk
1 cup sourdough starter
1 cup brown sugar
5 cups all-purpose flour
2 teaspoons baking soda
1 teaspoon salt
1 teaspoon cinnamon
2 eggs, beaten
2 tablepoons butter, melted

Blend milk, starter, and brown sugar, and set aside. Blend dry ingredients—flour, baking soda, salt, and cinnamon. Add

(*continued on following page*)

Just as exciting as the original bear sign was a yeast-raised version. More than likely, range cooks first made this from a sour-dough starter, giving the product a unique flavor.

While their version was sweet-ened with molasses, this is made with brown sugar for a sweeter taste.

BIRDS OF A FEATHER...

"Nesters" was the term given to Old West homesteaders, and they paid dearly for the opportunity to earn the name.

Until the spread of railroads, at least ninety percent of the country had never traveled farther than ten miles from home. Nesters were the exception. Striking out from neighborhood comforts, they would take as long as a year to move thousands of miles.

Nesters were required to comply with the Donation Land Act of 1850 and the Homesteading Act of 1862, which mandated building a home and living in it for at least five months out of the year, enclosing acreage (usually 160–320 acres) completely with two-wire fencing, sinking a well, constructing a water storage area, and cultivating a specified number of acres for crops—all this and surviving there for at least three to five years before title to the land could be granted.

beaten eggs and melted butter to the wet ingredients and stir. Stir in half the dry ingredients with a wooden spoon. When well blended, pour in the remaining dry ingredients, and knead until the dough is smooth and elastic like raw bread dough. Add more flour if necessary. Cover and let rise until double in bulk. Turn out on floured board or flat counter, and roll out to about ½–1 inch thick. Cut in strips or classic donut shapes and, once again, set aside on greased pan or waxed paper until double in bulk. Heat about 1 inch of oil to 375 degrees (a fresh bread cube will brown in oil in 1 minute at 375 degrees). Carefully, and the emphasis is on *carefully*, place the raw donuts into the hot skillet and brown on each side. Turn out on paper towels to cool.

Serve warm or cool with a topping of powdered sugar.

VARIATIONS

∽ Mix ½ cup of sugar with ¼ teaspoon cinnamon, and top donuts immediately upon removal from frying pan.

∽ For an authentic Old West flavor, substitute ½ cup molasses for brown sugar. Caution: it will not be very sweet.

Fruity Fritters

FRYING TIME: *1–2 minutes*

FRYING TEMPERATURE: *375 degrees*

1 cup whole milk

2 eggs, beaten

1 teaspoon lemon juice

2 tablepoons butter, melted

3 tablepoons granulated sugar

½ teaspoon salt

1½ cups all-purpose flour

3 cups fresh fruit

Mix all wet ingredients: milk, beaten eggs, lemon juice, and melted butter. Blend all dry ingredients and add to the wet mix. It should be the consistency of very thick spaghetti sauce. If not, add a bit more flour and blend; do not beat it in. Heat a large skillet with 1 inch of oil to 375 degrees. Cube and dry fruit on paper towels. Dip fruit into batter, then carefully into hot skillet. Turn out when browned and let cool.

Top with powdered sugar or a large scoop of ice cream.

VARIATIONS

~ Top with a mix of ½ cup sugar and ¼ teaspoon cinnamon.

~ Serve with fresh cream poured on top.

~ For a different flavor add a dash of nutmeg with dry ingredients.

Not far removed from what Native Americans did with their fresh harvest of berries, this recipe satisfies anyone's longing for a wonderful mix of fresh fruit and pastry. It's the Old West's version of a morning Danish.

Frybread

FRYING TIME: *15 seconds per side*
FRYING TEMPERATURE: *375 degrees*

3 cups all-purpose flour
1 tablespoon baking powder
1 teaspoon salt
1 teaspoon granulated sugar
1½ cups whole milk
2 tablepoons shortening, melted

 *ften thought of as a tradi-
tional Native American
food, it's been made by the tribes
of the Southwest only within the
last hundred years. It contains few
ingredients indigenous to the lands
of the Old West. Most frybread
ingredients came from the new
settlers and were acquired by tribes
through trading.*

*Development of this tasty
bread most likely happened as a
result of need by two cultures,
which found that frying bread in
a skillet could save time; the result
travelled well and lasted longer
than other breads.*

*There are as many recipes as
cooks. You can vary this recipe by
changing the size of the pieces—
or roll it out to ¾ inch thick, which
takes longer to fry but gives the
bread a chewier texture.*

*To impress onlookers, instead
of patting out the dough, pull a
piece twice the size of a golf ball,
form into a tortilla-like circle, and
shape by spinning and tossing it in
the air like a pizza. Although this
version is slower to shape, the family
dog will love what lands on the floor.*

Blend all four dry ingredients. Add the
milk and shortening, slowly stirring with
a wooden spoon. It will appear very dry.
Turn out on floured board or counter and
knead dough until firm, but don't overdo
it. Pat out the dough to about ¼ inch
thick. Cut into circles any size that will
fit the frying pan. Heat about 2 cups of
oil in your skillet to 375 degrees (a 1 inch
cube of bread will brown in 1 minute at
375 degrees). Carefully slide your dough
into the pan. The frybread should puff up
immediately. Turn once (very carefully)
when golden brown. Remove and drain
on paper towels.

Use frybread any way you can imagine. For example, fill with fruit and fold
over like a taco shell.

VARIATION

For a more authentic taste, delete
the sugar.

Houn' Ears & Whirlups

FRYING TIME: *1 minute*
FRYING TEMPERATURE: *375 degrees*

Houn' Ears:
>   2 cups sourdough starter
>   ½ cup water
>   1 teaspoon salt
>   1 teaspoon baking soda
>   1 tablespoon sugar
>   1–2 cups flour

Whirlup:
>   1 cup water
>   ½ cup sugar
>   ½ teaspoon cinnamon

Mix first five ingredients together. Add enough flour to make a thick batter. Drop tablespoonfuls into a hot pan of vegetable oil. Remove when brown.

For Whirlup, mix water and sugar together in a saucepan. Boil down until syrup forms. Remove and add cinnamon. Pour over Houn' Ears.

VARIATION
↪ Replace Whirlup with a more exotic version: Mix about 1 cup fresh fruit and 2 tablespoons sugar until liquid forms. Pour liquid into pan. Add another cup of water and ¼ cup sugar. Boil down to a syrup and add fruit. When all is warm, pour over fresh Houn' Ears.

riginating in New Mexico, Houn' Ears were made from a thin sourdough batter dropped by the spoonful into hot lard. As they fried brown, they generally fell into the shape of a dog's ear.

Whirlup was sugar-water sauce flavored with spices or chopped dried fruit. It was poured hot over the Houn' Ears and consumed on the spot.

A number of trail journals refer to Houn' Ears & Whirlups as the treat for the day. They were easy for chuck wagon cooks to blend and even quicker to cook.

Recipes vary as widely as the landscape. Whatever fruit or spice was available served as the base for the sauce.

Jolly Boys

bservant bakers may recognize Jolly Boys as a form of hush puppies, a round balls of cornmeal and sugar, but this is Old West–style with a touch of the ever-popular molasses.

Jolly Boys are another example of the adaptation of standard recipes found in the more civilized areas of the country. One can assume the name came from the illusion of a happy rotund male. Regardless, it should put a smile on your face to see the result piled on a bread tray with dinner.

They even can be used as a dessert topped with honey.

FRYING TIME: *5 minutes*

FRYING TEMPERATURE: *375 degrees*

¾ cup yellow cornmeal
4 tablepoons butter or margarine
1 cup buttermilk
¼ cup granulated sugar
2 tablepoons molasses
½ cup sourdough starter
3 eggs, beaten
1 teaspoon baking soda
2 cups all-purpose flour

Cook cornmeal in butter and buttermilk over low heat until meal is mushy. When still hot, add sugar and molasses; stir until dissolved. Cool, then add starter and mix well. Cover and set in a warm place overnight or until very light. The next day, add eggs, baking soda, and enough flour to make a fairly stiff batter. Make into balls the size of walnuts (use extra flour on hands, if necessary) and place on a floured cloth for about 1 hour. Fry in about 1 inch of oil at 375 degrees (a fresh bread cube will brown in oil in 1 minute at 375 degrees). Turn out on paper towels to cool.

When done, dust Jolly Boys with powered sugar and serve.

Jumbles

BAKING TIME: *10 minutes*
OVEN TEMPERATURE: *375 degrees*

1½ cups granulated sugar
¾ cup butter or margarine
3 tablepoons milk
3 eggs, beaten
1 teaspoon vanilla
½ teaspoon baking powder
½ teaspoon cream of tartar
3 cups all-purpose flour

Cream sugar and butter. Add milk, eggs, vanilla, and mix. In a separate bowl, blend baking powder, cream of tartar, and flour. Add to butter-egg mix and blend again. Drop by tablespoon onto a greased baking sheet. Top with powdered sugar if desired. Bake in preheated oven.

It's surprising that cookies were not very popular during the mid-nineteenth century. Some recipes were about, but few references were made to the baking and consumption of cookies in any numbers by pioneers, ranchers or cattle drivers. Perhaps it was too labor intensive to make individual servings of anything in such a rugged environment. They were not filling, nor did they provide any nourishment. Also, a delicate cookie didn't exactly fit any picture of the rugged West either, so I suspect they were probably not in any demand.

The closest to a cookie of any renown were jumbles. These were generally made in ranch homes in the late nineteenth century. Jumbles or "jumballs" were the precursor to butter-pressed cookies. Specially designed jumball presses, looking like a large tin syringe with inserts, made creative shapes.

However, few could afford the weight and room for the luxury of a jumball press aboard a covered wagon, so most jumbles were hand-pressed and cut, or dropped by tablespoon onto a baking sheet. They are very cakelike in texture.

Crackers: Crispy Treats

NFORTUNATELY, CRACKERS GAINED A VERY BAD REPUTATION IN THE Old West. Virtually all passages West included "sea biscuits" or "hardtack" on the menu. Hardtack was a thick cracker, void of moisture, that kept for years. It was as close to eating stone as one would ever want. The taste didn't compensate for the texture, for it too went away with the moisture. When weather was so foul a fire was impossible, or foodstuffs ran low, out came the hardtack. It was broken up and placed in cold stew, coffee, or even water to soften. Later, as pioneers settled in and supplies became easier to acquire, crackers replaced hardtack. Cracker manufacturing became a huge industry lasting into the twentieth century.

Unlike many other recipes, crackers call for complete evaporation of moisture while baking. To get thin, crispy crackers, here are a few helpful hints:

- Do not knead dough like bread. Developed gluten, so desirable in breads, is the worst thing that can happen to a cracker recipe.
- Start rolling assembled dough by patting it out with hands; then roll out on floured Formica or butcher block. Use a flat surface.
- The dough must be rolled out as thin as possible. About one-sixteenth of an inch is ideal. Do not overroll or you will develop the gluten.
- Try to roll out as evenly as possible to ensure uniform cracker size. This may take a few batches, but don't fret; they'll still be delicious.
- Poking holes in the crackers with a fork is decorative and prevents the dough from rising too far. But the holes must be deep to be effective.
- To add salt or other toppings, the top must be moist. Spray water or brush top with beaten egg or vegetable oil.
- To prevent soggy crackers, cool on a wire rack.

Pictured from top are Houn' Ears & Whirlups (page 159) and Soda Cracker Biscuit I (page 164).

Soda Cracker Biscuit I

This recipe was for those who had the time and inclination to make fresh crackers. Often old friends would bake up a huge batch for their departing neighbors traveling west. Each of these cracker recipes can be easily cut in half for your first couple of tries.

BAKING TIME: *10 minutes*
OVEN TEMPERATURE: *400 degrees*

4 cups all-purpose flour
2 teaspoons cream of tartar
4 tablepoons butter or margarine
1 teaspoon baking soda
1 teaspoon salt
2 cups buttermilk

Sift the flour with the cream of tartar and cut in the butter. Dissolve soda and salt in milk, and mix into soft dough. Knead until elastic. Roll out wafer-thin. Fold over and roll again. Place on a greased cookie sheet and cut into squares. Prick them all over. Bake in hot oven about 20 minutes or until dry. Cool on wire rack.

Soda Cracker Biscuit II

BAKING TIME: *10 minutes*
OVEN TEMPERATURE: *400 degrees*

4 cups all-purpose flour
2 teaspoons cream tartar
1 cup butter or margarine
2 cups water
1½ teaspoons baking powder

Thoroughly mix the flour with the cream of tartar. Cut in butter. Add water and baking powder together. Knead until elastic. Let rest about 10 minutes. Roll out wafer-thin. Fold over once and roll out again. Place on well-greased cookie sheet and cut into squares. Prick them all over. Bake in hot oven about 10 minutes or until dry. Cool on wire rack.

SERVING TIPS FROM A CAMPFIRE MASTER

A cook didn't always know how many would show up at any given meal. He did his best to serve everyone, but sometimes would have to resort to a few old tricks.

One chuck wagon cook related a maneuver that only someone of his seasoning could conjure. If it appeared more were surrounding the chuck wagon than he had prepared for, rather than removing the food vessels from the fire, he set them in a hot trench filled with red coals. This required cowboys to reach over an excruciatingly hot fire to dip for their meal. Few would spend much time scooping because the intense heat hit them directly in the face; they rarely filled their plates.

This undoubtedly stroked every mischievous bone in the cook's body.

FUEL FOR THE FIRE

Unfortunately, the desert landscape rarely provided enough fuel for range stoves, Franklin stoves, or campfires. In abundance, though, were cattle and buffalo— and the by-products of months of grazing. In the pioneer spirit of making do, this "anthracite of the desert" burned nicely when dried. Wheelbarrow-loads of cow and buffalo chips made their way to ranch houses to dehydrate, harden, and be used as fuel.

Chuck wagons often predicated their daily setup on the numbers of "piles" surrounding the campsite for easy access.

Cooking with "prairie fuel" was not easy. After being dried, it burned so fast that it was difficult to control and required one to constantly stoke the fire.

At first, new bakers and cooks were very discreet in handling the fuel. One can assume they were not particularity proud of the source of this necessity. However, as time passed, they handled chips like piles of dirty laundry, gathered by arm loads and stacked before fires for later use. One person was assigned the task of fire-feeding throughout the evening.

There is no documentation on the flavoring this may have added to foods. Rest assured, we will not attempt to duplicate it here.

Breakfast Foods: Starting the Day

W HETHER EATEN BY PIONEERS MOVING WEST IN A WAGON train or by cattle drivers moving north with their chuck wagons in tow, breakfast on the trail was one of the day's highlights.

Wagon train mornings usually started by stoking the fire, long burned down from the night before. While the man of the wagon went to the fields to gather up the oxen, the woman started breakfast in the midst of packing for the day's travel. Cattle driving mornings were a bit different. At least a few cowboys were always awake to watch herds, and fires were constantly burning to keep the coffee warm. "Cookie" also started breakfast and packed for the day at first light.

What wagon train and chuck wagon cooks had in common were the kind of foods they served. By far the most popular breakfast was flapjacks, slapjacks, or griddle cakes. They were generally one and the same—a flour and water mass baked on a griddle with lard, butter or a concoction called "Charlie Taylor." "Charlie Taylor" was a butter substitute made of a sorghum and bacon grease mix. Now if that doesn't take your breath away . . .

Most griddle cakes were made with sourdough for taste, and baking soda or saleratus for leavening. To ripen sourdough flavor, the mix was often assembled the evening before. The secret according to one nineteenth-century baker was "batters so thin they can be dropped by spoon onto a hot griddle . . . a cold griddle will make the griddle cakes tough, unpalatable and very unwholesome."

So, to try a palatable, wholesome griddle cake tomorrow morning, here's an assortment of Old West styles you're sure to enjoy.

Note: All batters should stir like thick gravy. Add extra flour as necessary.

Buckwheat Griddle Cakes

1 cup sourdough
2 cups water
1 teaspoon salt
2 tablepoons molasses
2 cups buckwheat flour
1 teaspoon baking soda

Mix all except baking soda and set in warm place overnight. In the morning, put in soda, stirring lightly. Do not beat. Pour or ladle onto hot griddle. Turn over when bubbles form on top of the griddle cakes.

Cornmeal Griddle Cakes

1 cup water
1 teaspoon salt
2 cups sourdough
1 cup cornmeal
1 teaspoon baking soda

Mix all except baking soda and set in warm place overnight. In the morning, put in soda, stirring lightly. Do not beat. Pour or ladle onto hot griddle. Turn over when bubbles form on top of the griddle cakes.

Rice Griddle Cakes

2 cups cooked rice
2 cups whole milk
2 eggs, beaten
1 teaspoon salt
2 cups whole wheat flour
1 teaspoon baking soda

Soak rice in milk overnight. In the morning, add eggs, salt, and flour to thicken. Stir and pour or ladle onto hot griddle. Turn over when bubbles form on top of the griddle cakes.

Bread Griddle Cakes

6 slices dry bread
2 cups buttermilk
4 eggs, beaten
1 teaspoon baking soda
½ teaspoon salt
2 cups all-purpose flour

Break dry bread into crumbs and soak overnight in buttermilk. Add beaten eggs, baking soda, and salt. Thicken with flour, about 2 cups. Pour or ladle onto hot griddle. Turn over when bubbles form on top of the griddle cakes.

MAYOR ON THE RANGE

The most popular place for cowboys to rest after sixteen to eighteen hours on the range mingling with cattle was around the chuck wagon campfire. Cowpokes would eat, socialize, and sleep within forty feet of this instant community, and it was understood that the cook was the leader as long as the campfire burned.

His wagon carried most of the important goods necessary for a comfortable trip. It included extra bedding, medicine, sewing material, ammunition, and anything else he deemed appropriate to run the show. Of course, someone had to dispense these items, so "Cookie" was the trail drive seamstress, doctor, dentist, barber, and purveyor of commissary goods. He was also the law, controlling any trail hand disagreements.

(continued on page 170)

(continued from page 169)

His leverage for enforce-ment of all trail drive codes wasn't in his muscle, but in his cooking. For better or worse, he was the only option for a hungry cowhand. If the cowhand wanted to eat, he would take great pains to stay on the good side of the cattle drive's appointed mayor.

Splatter Dabs

1 cup sourdough starter
1 cup all-purpose flour
1 egg, beaten
1½ cups whole milk
½ teaspoon salt
2 tablespoons butter, melted
1 teaspoon baking soda
1 tablespoon granulated sugar

Mix all and beat. Pour or ladle onto hot griddle. Turn over when bubbles form on top of the splatter dabs.

Shorty Harris cooking at his desert camp.

Corn-Doggie Flapjacks

2 cups all-purpose flour
1 tablespoon baking powder
1 tablespoon granulated sugar
½ teaspoon salt
1 can creamed corn (8-ounces)
1 tablespoon butter, melted
½ cup water

Blend the dry ingredients—flour, baking powder, sugar, and salt. Add creamed corn (using all the canned liquid), melted butter, and water. Stir to mix, but do not overmix. Grease a hot skillet with solid shortening and pour a scoop of the mix to test the temperature. Bubbles should form on top of the flapjack before turning. Brown on both sides and serve.

VARIATIONS
⌁ Sprinkle with powdered sugar prior to serving.
⌁ Use honey as a topping instead of the usual syrup.

A special treat and change of pace from the usual bill of fare, Corn-Doggie Flapjacks could be made just about anywhere because of the relatively "new" canning process. Having goods handy in cans allowed mixing many items normally not mixed because of seasonal availability.

This turns out to be a chunky corn bread–like pancake and is very delicious.

GETTIN' THE GRIDDLE READY

Smoothing a new griddle simply requires putting a teaspoon of salt on it when hot, rubbing it with brown paper, then heavily greasing the top. Rub the grease off with a dry cloth, wash it clean, and it's ready to use.

Bibliography

Adams, Andy. 1903. *The Log of a Cowboy*. Williamstown, Md.: Crown House.

Adams, Ramon F. 1952. *Come an' Get It*. Norman, Okla.: Univ. of Oklahoma Press.

Beitz, Les. 1968. *Treasury of Frontier Relics*. New York: Edwin House.

Cook, Harold J. 1968. *Tales of the 04 Ranch*. Lincoln, Neb.: Univ. of Nebraska Press.

Dale, Edward E. 1965. *Cow Country*. Norman, Okla.: Univ. of Oklahoma Press.

Dick, Everett. 1954. *The Sod-House Frontier*. Lincoln, Neb.: Johnsen.

Dobie, J. Frank. 1964. *Cow People*. Boston: Little Brown and Company.

Faulk, Odie B. 1963. *Land of Many Frontiers*. New York: Oxford Univ. Press.

Ferris, Robert G. 1967. *Prospector, Cowhand, and Sodbuster*. Washington DC: U.S. Dept. of the Interior.

Forbis, William H. 1973. *The Cowboys*. New York: Time-Life Books.

Haley, James L. 1982. *Apaches*. New York: Doubleday.

Horn, Hudson. 1974. *The Pioneers*. New York: Time-Life Books.

Kennedy, Marguerite Wallace. 1951. *My Home on the Range*. Boston: Little, Brown and Company.

Kirlin, Katherine and Thomas Kirlin. 1991. *Smithsonian Folklife Cookbook*. Washington DC: Smithsonian Institution Press.

Luchetti, Cathy and Carol Olwell. 1982. *Women of the West*. New York: Orion Books.

Mrs. Cronkite's Cook Book. 1885. Sacramento: E. W. Here

Niethammer, Carolyn. 1974. *American Indian Food and Lore*. New York: Macmillan.

The CO Bar chuck wagon, near Cedar Ranch, Arizona Territory, August 5, 1908.

Perl, Lila. 1965. *Red-Flannel Hash and Shoo-Fly Pie*. Cleveland, Ohio: World Publishing.

Ragsdale, John G. 1991. *Dutch Ovens Chronicled*. Fayetteville, Ark.: Univ. of Arkansas Press.

Savage, William W. 1973. *Cowboy Life*. Norman, Okla.: Univ. of Oklahoma Press.

Soule, Gardner. 1976. *The Long Trail*. New York: McGraw-Hill.

Tannahill, Reay. 1988. *Food in History*. New York: Crown.

Schlissel, Lillian. 1982. *Women's Diaries of the Westward Journey*. New York: Schocken Books.

Index

Page numbers in *italic* refer to photographs.

WHEN LON WALTERS WAS A CHILD, HIS PARENTS QUICKLY DISCOVERED THAT HE would eat anything if it were served with bread and butter or if some kind of dessert were offered. Of course, this gave his parents virtually unlimited leverage over his actions.

For several years the possibility of getting cut off from his bread and dessert habit persuaded Lon to behave. He soon realized, however, that it was far more productive to learn mixing and baking. And so his career as a baker began.

Lon cooked for recreation during his lengthy career as an aviator in the U.S. Navy, and opened a large bakery in San Diego, California, after retiring from the service. Lon and his staff created uniquely wonderful products, things not created in a normal bakery. They didn't accept that something couldn't be done.

It was this "nothing is impossible" philosophy that led him to study Old West baking. Pioneers and Native Americans did so much with so little that he became fascinated about how respectable baked goods could be created on the open range.

Lon curently lives in Sedona with his wife, Margi. He writes a weekly food column for the *Sedona Red Rock News,* and baking continues to fill his spare time.